L♥VE IN THE 5TH DIMENSION

Ianneia Livia Silke Meldgaard

Published in 2023 by EMPOWER YOU

ISBN Paperback: 978-87-972739-4-4
Ebook: 978-87-972739-3-7

Published with the help of indie authors world
www.indieauthorsworld.com

This book wanted to be written.

And it asked: *Do you want to write me? Because Love wants to express itself.*

And I said yes.

I dedicate this book to all humans
who choose to follow the path of their soul,
regardless of the prize.

A Shift for Mother Earth

And for You and I

This book is about Love. But why is it called *Love in the 5th Dimension*? Isn't Love the same, regardless of which dimension we are in? And what is the thing with all those dimensions again?

First of all, yes. Love as a universal energy is, at its core, unchangeable. It is the origin of everything in the universe — you and me alike — and thus the energy tethering everything together. And like that, it is the most constant thing to exist.

Quite simply, Love *is*.

But the way we understand and practice Love here on Earth changes. We haven't had access to the spiritual dimensions our souls derive from, which consist of unconditional Love, here on our physical Earth as there has been a dense veil between worlds. Because of this, and the consequential absence of unconditional Love, we have had to "rediscover" our understanding and interpretation of Love in our earthly lives.

In reality, this might have been the very meaning of life on Earth up until now, that our souls have desired to reach a more profound experience of Love's true nature by living in a dimension where the direct connection to the source is absent. This rediscovery and reclamation of Love has allowed us to sharpen our awareness and appreciation of its deeper qualities — the same way that an absence of light sharpens our awareness and appreciation of *its* qualities.

This brings us on to the second question, which is about those dimensions. This is a special time because we are standing in the middle of a shift, where Mother Earth is moving from what we call the 3rd dimension to the 5th dimension (from now on, 3D and 5D). You might have heard of the paradigm shift, the shift from the Piscean Age to the Aquarian Age — or the shift from the 3rd to the 5th dimension. No matter what we call it, the Earth is moving from one dimension with low vibrations and thus a dense veil between the physical and spiritual world; to a dimension with higher vibrations and a thinner veil between the physical and spiritual world. This shift is touching all of humankind and all other life on the planet.

As Earth's vibrations rise, the vibrations in every individual human and the shared human consciousness do, too. And this doesn't happen quietly. All of the turmoil we are experiencing in the world at this time is a result of the vibrational rise that the Earth and human race are experiencing. We are moving as a collective and as individuals into a clearer dimension where the new and higher vibrations are shining a light on everything from the past. It is challenging us to take a stand on whether or not we want to carry this with us into our new lives in 5D — or if it needs upgrading. It is obvious when we look around us that a lot of what we, up until now in our 3D life, have viewed as normal and natural — or at least something necessary to "learn to live with"

— suddenly sparks discussion because it doesn't sit right with us anymore.

This also goes for Love. Or perhaps we should say that it *especially* goes for Love since it, as stated, is the origin of everything and is thus the energy that tethers everything together. So, our way of understanding and practising Love is essential to our lives. There are many elements of the old perception of Love that now — with the rising vibrations and a clearer consciousness — is up for re-evaluation.

In these years, we are noticing aspects of Love that we previously have not. The most fundamental aspect is that Love isn't a limited resource, but an infinite source that constantly runs through us. As mentioned, we haven't had direct access to that source in 3D due to the veil. So, while present in low vibrations, the true essence of Love has only been reachable for those few enlightened who have dedicated their lives to the search. In 5D, the awareness of Love as an infinite resource is accessible to us all, which naturally presents a need for a new pair of eyes to look at our way of understanding and practising Love.

Additionally, we are now beginning to understand that one of the most essential prerequisites for true compassion is that we love ourselves, because it is precisely self-Love that is the key to opening up the infinite source of Love. It didn't look like that in 3D, where loving oneself was, to a great extent, perceived negatively as excessive self-centredness. This perception is deeply rooted inside of all of our subconscious because it has been reaffirmed over and over again — by religion, society, and passing through generations. It is one of those "twists of love" (as it will be referred to in this book) that truly needs an upgrade at the threshold of 5D.

When it comes to Love in our relationships at this time, we are also beginning to understand that we, for the most part, are unable to give anything to others that we ourselves don't have. And we can't attract something we don't already have inside ourselves. So, the quality of the relationship we have with ourselves fully determines our relationships with others. That is why the act of enhancing the Love for yourself fills most of this book's pages. It constitutes the foundation of your life in 5D, and your ability to let Love flow between you and others.

The Structure of This Book

In Chapter 1, you will read the history of Love that I — as a Danish, West-European woman, with my own personal love story as a child in Denmark's '60s — can tell you about, and the twisted love and childhood trauma that ensued. My childhood experiences meant that early on I developed a strong sense of responsibility, co-dependency, and an introjective personality, conditioned to love others more than myself.

The first thirty years of my adult life have focused on disentangling the twisted love and reclaiming true Love. And from this, create and live an authentic life that's connected to my soul. This process has simultaneously been a journey from 3D consciousness, where the ego reigns, to 5D consciousness, where the soul's awareness of how things are connected is essential.

I have lived many experiences in this process, which lays the foundations for this book. In Chapters 2-5, I present different ways to disentangle your personal twisted love to upgrade your ability to love, first of all yourself. In all of these chapters, you will gain insight into the topics at hand and tools, exercises, and tips to anchor the insight as a life-changing power. So you can slowly — or quickly, depending on your temperament — elevate your vibrations on the course of true and unconditional Love within yourself and thus your life.

Because *your life is as you are*. When you are filled with Love, your life will be, too. When you undo your twisted love from 3D, and as your system comes into tune with the true essence of Love, you will follow on Mother Earth's journey into 5D. In harmony with your planet, you can relish the possibilities the new and higher vibrations provide for us.

In the last chapter, we will go over everything and look at how it all connects in 5D's unity consciousness.

I hope you enjoy the book and the journey of opening yourself up to even more Love in your life.

Note

Now you might be sitting there with a very relevant question: What about the 4th dimension — or 4D? What happened to that one? It is a question I often get when I talk with people about the shifting of dimensions. You will get the ultrashort answer:

4D is a dimension where a variety of levels and worlds exist, including what we often refer to as the *astral plane*. Consciousness-wise, we move through 4D on our way to 5D, which is where a lot of the turmoil and confusion we are currently experiencing stems from. Right now, we are experiencing the last compulsions of the old fear-based world as the new Love-based world is gaining more and more momentum. You can say that this between-worlds fighting is taking place in 4D. We have opened up to a new and much more nuanced way of perceiving ourselves and life on Earth than what we have known from 3D. But we have not yet landed in 5D where we have realised the illusions, thus seeing and feeling the truth clearly. So right now we are in a kind of 4D-wilderness where everything is up in the air. But since the goal for Mother Earth's and humankind's current ascension is to get to 5D, it is 5D's Love qualities we are aiming for in the process of elevating our vibrations — and thus this is the topic of this book.

CHAPTER 1

A Story About Love

A Historic View on Collective and Personal Love-Stories

et me begin by expanding a bit on the previously mentioned paradigm shift that we are currently going through, so Love can express itself from a proper foundation. Regardless of what we call the shift, it means that our understanding of nearly everything is going through a transformation. At the same time, it offers many opportunities for healing and transforming ancient patterns and blocks, individually and collectively. You might have noticed that both within yourself and in the people around you that many healing conversations and processes are taking place. That's because this time allows for completely unique opportunities for healing, and a lot of souls have chosen to put an end to several karmic themes in this life.

We are in the middle of one of the characteristics of these healing processes — the transformation of fundamental fear which has dominated life in 3D. This fear erupts from the ego's perception that it is separate from others and that, because of this, it has to protect itself and those closest to it. While the ego at the same time operates from a sense of scarcity that there isn't enough for all — enough of Love, food, money, attention, room, etc. — and that oneself is, fundamentally, not (good) enough. So, the ego finds itself in a constant state of alertness.

Here on the threshold of 5D, we start to notice that the fear and perception of separation is actually an illusion. As the vibrations rise and the veil between life on Earth and the spiritual dimensions thin, we will get closer in touch with our souls and, through that, the deeper truth about life and ourselves. The soul operates from a foundation that vibrates on a higher frequency than that of the ego, where the essential feelings are Love and trust to the kind and generous universe, where there is enough for all, and where we are all wholly perfect and valued, exactly as we are. In addition to that, the soul knows that we are all connected in a way where what I do for myself affects the whole in a positive way — the same way that the good I do for others will come back to me in a positive way.

What is so special about the energy shift we are in the middle of — which we also call the ascension process — is that the shift from ego to soul-consciousness happens while we are still in our physical body. Right now, and in the years to come — all depending on the pace we each decide to go through the process in — we will be reborn in a way that can be compared to the shift we have previously experienced, when we go through the process of death and leave the physical body.

You might have heard or read about people that have had near-death experiences where, as they leave their physical body, they experience a shift from Earth's limited awareness to a larger and clearer awareness. A shift where they see themselves and their lives from a higher perspective; where the truth and the inter-connectedness of everything is suddenly crystal clear, and where there is an unconditionally loving view of everything. An example of this is Anita Moorjani, one of the biggest self-Love teachers of contemporary times, and someone I constantly find myself coming back to. Her book, *Dying to be Me*, is about her own near-death experience.

This is actually the type of shift that's happening on Earth right now — although not in the dated notion of death where we are leaving our physical body, but where we are still present as physical beings on the planet. We are learning to view ourselves and each other with the loving and empathetic eyes of the soul, instead of the judgemental and evaluative eyes of the ego that we are so used to. It isn't necessarily an easy process, but it is still fundamental as we step into our new life in 5D.

From the Hippie Movement to the Paradigm Shift

The paradigm shift has been underway for several years. As you will see when you get to *The Love Story of the Past Century* section, life in the western world has gone through a dramatic development in the past four to five generations — and, consequentially, so have the conditions of Love.

In the 1960s and '70s, we experienced a temporary boiling point of this development with the youth revolt and women's liberation's tsunami of insurgency against the old and constraining chains. We can in many ways view what happened in the '70s as the precursor to the big paradigm shift that is becoming a reality now, in the

2020s. The youth revolt and counter-culture against authority, the hippie movement's messages about *peace-love-and-harmony*, and the women's liberations' insistence on equal rights were all huge milestones in the movement from the old mindset of 3D to the new mindset of 5D.

If we look at Love, which is the overarching theme of this book, then the hippie movement's inspiration of a more loving, open-minded, and peaceful co-existence — with everything that followed from it, such as new child pedagogy, a new view on relationships, a wave of emotionally liberating therapy, etc. — is the most important sign of new times. When they sung about *The Age of Aquarius* in the late '60s musical *Hair*, it wasn't a coincidence, but rather because this period opened up for a peek at the energy we were heading towards with the paradigm shift, and that the hippie movement got a taste of. A taste that they could now pass on to the rest of humankind.

From the hippie movement, a new-age consciousness grew which would become a wide tide, spreading into several different directions and that, up until this very day, has had a very big influence on the shift of the human consciousness that has been taking place, and is currently reaching its climax. But why would it climax now, in 2020? And why is there a need for a discussion about Love's true being now, fifty years after the hippies and the new age movement pointed out *peace-love-and-harmony* as the new form of life? Because a paradigm shift takes a long time. There are many phases underway, and the opening to the new energy we experienced in the '70s needed to go through the layers of the old paradigm. It needed to be turned and twisted, misunderstood, distorted, upgraded, polished, and looked at from one side and then the other. We are now ready to leap and seriously take the new consciousness to heart, and begin to understand how a trusting, loving, peace-based approach to life on planet Earth can actually be implemented in practice.

Love and Gender Roles

One of the layers that the new understanding of Love needed to go through was the layer of the age-old gender roles. Most of the individuals who have carried the Love-energy in the new age movement forward in life in the past fifty years have been women. In the 2020s, you still can't attend a yoga class, spiritual seminar, or workshop with various so-called "alternative" healing-modalities without 80%, often even 90%, of the attend-ants being women. And it makes a lot of sense considering Love has, in many ways, been a traditionally feminine domain. In this day and age, it is also the case that we often deem the new energy as feminine energy. Not to be mis-understood as the energy itself only consisting of feminine qualities — the energy vibrations in 5D in its essence contains an equal and balanced core of both feminine and masculine qualities. That we call the new energy feminine should instead be understood in the sense that we, to balance the enormous imbalance of masculine perspective and prioritisation that the past six thousand years of pa-

*peace, love
and
harmony*

triarchy has left us with, have presented a need for a heavy dose of feminine energy to carry us into the new times. We have received this through the many female frameworks of perception and prioritisation, e.g., in the new age movement.

But what happened to the flow of Love-energy when it was set free amongst the hippie and the new age movement's many women of the '60s, '70s, and '80s, including myself? We, of course, got it to fit within our pre-established structure of perception as we humans always do when something new comes our way. It is one of the conditions of human development: Everything new will get its place in our system, on the condition that we can make it fit within our known and established structure. That's why true evolvement takes such a long time, and why quantum leaps and paradigm shifts are connected with so much pain and resistance — because in changes of that size we *also* have to change the very foundation of our structures of perception, which most of us don't "just do" without a fight.

So, the new liberation of women's lives and Love in many ways unfolded within the structure of the previously known gender roles. The principles of the patriarchal society — upheld by the cultural and religious view of women and men — still played a large role in both men and women's interpretations of the new opportunities and principles of life. We were all given these by our parents and previous generations, and they lived with content in the subconscious worlds from where our lives and behaviours are controlled.

In terms of Love, this meant that the traditional knowledge of Love as a sacrificial quality with most focus on compassion for *the other* — as women for generations were taught — became the foundation the revolution of Love built itself on. Societal norms and systems innately limited *how* innovative and revolutionary the energy waves of the '70s could be. In addition, each and every one of us who, in different ways, became ambassadors for the new understanding of Love also carried with us personal trauma and wounds — or as I call them in this book, *twists of love* — that we naturally also carried with us into the revolt against old edicts. Subconscious patterns that stemmed from our own upbringing, and that — regardless of how liberated we were on a conscious level — controlled our Love-patterns and behaviourisms to a degree that many of us, now middle-aged, are surprised by as we look back at our lives. More on that later, when we get to my personal love story.

Said in a different way: When 5D's energy first knocked on the '70s earthbound society, it was overall understood and practiced from a 3D mindset. Fifty years would go by before we are now ready for the actual quantum leap, and to seriously understand the depth of what the new energy is bringing us. A radical change is needed to implement this energy. Both when it comes to Love and when it comes to the equality between all people regardless of gender, skin colour, culture, sexuality, and social status. The current second wave of feminism and the many equal rights-movements that are currently happening across the world — with a demand for respect and acknowledgement of all people — are showing us the next steps right now as the new energy is settling on Earth.

The rest of this book is focused on the new interpretations of Love that we are ready to take on, and which the new energy lovingly guides us to look at in our own lives. We will look at the aspects of Love that need the most upgrade before we can step into our new life in the new energy. And most importantly, we will look at how you can practise Love on a higher frequency that's in better harmony with your and Love's true essence.

The Love Story of the Past Century

But before we get to that, let's take a quick look at the past century's love story as it has played out in mine and my ancestors' lives in Denmark. There are, of course, many stories to tell from other parts of the world beyond West-European Denmark, but since that is where my ancestors and I have lived, that's the story I can tell you. What conditions of Love were given to my generation from the one that came before? And what have we passed on? As mentioned earlier, over the past one hundred years there have been vast developments from one generation to another. The terms and conditions for living on Earth in the western culture have changed considerably. And while our understanding and practice of Love has had to adjust to the circumstances of life people have been put through, then the conditions of Love have also changed remarkably.

There aren't many from my parents' generation who don't carry a variety of emotional wounds and trauma with them in their luggage. They came from a childhood in the 1920s and '30s where poverty and having little means was the circumstance for most. Survival was high on the priority list. And when survival takes up a lot of space, it is necessary to close off the finer, more sensitive layers within oneself and one's children. Sensitivity usually clashes with the necessary tough work to meet the basic needs. Unconditional Love and empathy in that regard was a luxury that only few could indulge. Love had to be twisted for survival.

In the 1950s and '60s, when my generation was born and raised, prosperity and wellness emerged. My parents' generation was then given time and space to take more care of themselves and their children than their parents had been able to. But because of the childhood trauma they endured, they didn't have the emotional resources needed to sense and meet the frailer layers of their children's needs. So the negligence of sensitivity remained, even if slightly less tough. And the wounds on people's souls lived on, despite being incorporated in new versions. The twisted love continued its path on Earth, only slightly less constrained. The same applies to the relationship between my generation and our children. We pass on our predecessors' patterns but are opening up ever so slightly for more Love and empathy as the chains loosen and we get wiser to the true needs of both children and adults. The childhood trauma that most who grew up in the

'80s and '90s carry with them are, in many ways, of the same root of earlier generations, just not as firmly enforced. The new-energy-tsunami of the '70s furthermore shook the darkness living in the unconscious and formed a long list of tools to heal emotional wounds and trauma — tools that a large part of my own generation and my children's have employed.

This means that the grandchildren of my generation who are currently growing up will now have way better opportunities to experience the true, untwisted Love and empathy from their parents. There are simply not as many demons at play in family relations regarding undiscovered and unresolved emotional trauma that stands in the way of a parent's unconditional Love for their child.

So now, as we are approaching the threshold of the new age, there is finally hope that Love's true essence can extend itself as the foundation for our interactions with one another, first and foremost in close family relations where our concepts of Love are created. Exactly as all parents, without a doubt, have always felt a longing for, but haven't had the ability for. And when this first begins to show, there are no limits as to how much life on Earth can change. Love is the essence of everything — everything we are, and everything there is — and when this essence is allowed to express itself in its true, untwisted form, magic and miracles will find their way into our individual and collective lives, in a way that our 3D consciousness can't even comprehend.

In the following section, you will gain insight into how the described twisted love has unveiled itself in my life — which concrete lesson on Love lay in my subconscious as a result of some very specific twists of love from my parents, that they had been gifted from their own parents? Even though every family is, of course, unique in its ways of twisting love, I do believe that you will resonate with some of these elements. And if not, perhaps my story will awaken some memories that you can use as momentum for your own process in untangling your own twisted love.

My Love Story

I grew up in a very ordinary middle-class family in Denmark in the 1960s and '70s. My parents had — like every other family — their unique variants of the patterns I described earlier. Their own special ways of twisting Love; their subtle way of suffocating sensibility. Their personal emotional trauma that naturally carried over to their parenting skills when it came to my sister and me.

My mother was the youngest of six sisters. She had patterns from her childhood which meant she had difficulty controlling her emotional reactions. In many ways, she was a frustrated and caged woman. She was educated as a trilingual correspondent and had a good job in the travel sector, until she got married and had children at thirty years old. Her intelligence and abilities called for much more than being a housewife. But that was what the era expected of married women with young children. So that was what my mother did until

*love is the
essence of
everything*

I, the youngest, began school. This role as a housewife unleashed a lot of frustrations, mood swings, and "bad nerves" in my mother's character. It meant that I, as a child, would often experience a side of her that confused me and made me feel unsafe. Had I done something wrong? Was there a problem? Was I the cause of her bad mood, her rage, her frustrations?

My father was the third out of four siblings. He was a loving man that I had a deep connection with. In contrast to my mother, he was in better balance with himself and the life that society expected of him. He worked outside of the home — like most men at the time — and that alone gave him status and many opportunities to live out his desires and dreams, thus keeping his inner demons at bay. At the same time, as he was out of the home, he was also allowed to stay out of the daily interactions with the children and the emotional challenges this naturally would give rise to.

I was — and am — not in doubt as to whether my parents loved me or not. But I am also not in doubt as to the different ways Love was twisted in my family, and the consequences that has had on my wellbeing and my ability to create a gratifying life for myself. The personal development that I have worked on for more than thirty years to reach an inner connection with true Love, has taught me how the dysfunctional patterns from my childhood have followed me throughout my life and prevented me from stretching my wings fully. In the following, I will use an episode from my childhood to describe the most important dysfunctions. The episode contains most of the central twists of love that I have fought with my entire adult life.

My Mother Loses It

I am seven years old. It's bedtime. I am lying in bed and my dad sits next to me, tucking me into bed. We are fooling around and joking, playing, and tickling, and I am laughing and whining with glee and ecstasy. A moment in time, where unrestrained happiness and childlike joy fills the room and me. A feeling of surrender to bliss.

Suddenly, my mother stands by the doorframe. She is raging. She yells loudly and is throwing a wealth of accusations towards my dad and me. I don't remember the exact words she used, but it was about how we/my dad had done something terribly wrong. On how our relationship was too close, on how some lines had been crossed. On how we/I were at fault.

There is nothing about the situation that makes me think any lines were crossed by my dad. I only think of freedom, and I remember the feelings of glee and bliss inside of me. But in my mother's view, it looked completely different. Her frustrations and jealousy of the close bond my dad and I shared made her world fall apart that evening. She could no longer bear her own sorrow of unresolved longings. The glass overflowed and she let it all out on my dad and me.

I was paralysed. Laying in my bed, not even daring to breathe. Shock. The heavy feeling in the chest of having done something really bad. The feeling of guilt.

And confusion as to what it was that I had done. What was wrong? How did I fail? How had I sinned? If I were to judge from my mother's reaction, it was a very serious sin.

My dad tried to calm my mother down. It was impossible. He stood up, and together they went into the living room to untangle the threads. And I was left, alone in my bed. With the shock, numbness, guilt, and confusion. It was nearly impossible to move away from. What had happened — what I had done — was so serious that it felt impossible to live with.

I fell asleep. The next morning as my family woke up, it was as if nothing had happened at all. Kindness. Welcoming. Breakfast. Just as usual. The day went ahead. Nobody came to me.

Nobody said:

How are you doing?

I'm sorry about what happened yesterday.

Are you OK?

Did you sleep afterwards?

That was pretty intense, I am sorry you had to experience that.

I understand if you were scared.

It, of course, had nothing to do with you.

You haven't done anything wrong.

It was mine/mum's own frustration, I/she let it out on you.

It wasn't fair.

I am sorry.

Nobody said anything close to that. I carried the responsibility of that experience inside of me. I was seven years old.

And we all went on. We had to. I have always had an enhanced version of the survival strategy we call *get back on the horse*. As most children have. It is that which keeps us alive in those situations where we are about to die. Emotionally or physically. There are many children that have carried — and carry — experiences that are much more traumatising than what I described. Because it's necessary. Because they have no choice if they want to survive.

So, I carried that energy — within myself and my family. I tried to fix the horrible thing I had done by being happy, joking around, and not being a burden. I managed quite well and got very good at using my head. I am sure that my parents thought about that episode every now and then, looked at me, and assured themselves that I had forgotten all about it. I had moved on. We had all moved on.

That was fifty-six years ago. And the twisted love that we created in our family, like that episode, has ingrained itself in my subconscious ever since. The twists my parents created, because they couldn't do anything else. Because they had no idea what they should do about that episode. And because they thought, as many did at the time, that time heals all wounds. It would only make it worse to speak with the child about what had happened — even experts believed that back then. The twisted love that was ingrained in my system that night defined my adult love life for twenty to thirty years. Up until a few years ago when the work I had done on myself finally resulted in my ability to disentangle it. Before we continue on with the insights and tools which made that possible — which is the rest of this book — let me summarise what I learned about Love that night, when I was seven years old.

I Especially Learned These Three Lessons:

a. I learned that the people I have the closest, most loving bonds with are allowed to abuse me. If they can't cope with their own pain, then it is OK for them to project it onto me. Feeling like I had to carry other people's pain became a circumstance of life for me. It constituted a large part of close relationships for me. Fluid lines between *you and me* and *what is my stuff and what is yours* became part of being in intimate relationships. I became a *woman who loved too much*, so much so that I exhausted my system by carrying too many burdens that weren't my own. My Love life became a co-dependent relationship.

b. I learned that when I gave myself to the free flow of life's energy and experienced glee, fun, and bliss, then horrible things could happen. What I experienced as a pure and safe expression of Love could be turned on its head. I was guilty of something very serious, but I never figured out what it was. It meant that throughout my adult life, I have been on my toes. Whenever something became too good, I was prepared for the rug to be pulled out from under my feet. Which has then also happened because we create what we believe deep down in our sub-conscious. And when the rug was pulled and Love was — again — entangled, a voice in my subconscious would tell me, *"It is probably your fault. It is you that has to change. It is you that has done something wrong; you that has to be careful next time."*

c. And I learned that when someone has treated me unfairly, inappropriately, and unlovingly, then I could nor should not expect them to pick up the pieces. I had no right to expect that they would come back once the situation had calmed down and express any care for what emotions their behaviour had un-leashed in me. I just had to figure out how to move on. My restlessness, grief, and anger was not important enough that I, or anyone else, should bother taking care of it. I had to just *get back up on the horse*. And as I got older and started to demand that people who hurt me came back and made amends if I were to have anything more to do with them, then I did it with a commanding anger. Because deep down, I didn't believe that I had any right to do so. So, the discussions I had with them were really an expression of my inner discussion with myself as to whether it was now in order for me to claim that right. I was not able to set healthy boundaries for myself in a peaceful manner.

A lot of love-twists were created that night. Twists that I — as mentioned — have worked to undo my entire life. The perceptions of Love that I have lived out are pretty far from the true expression of Divine Love. I am sure you can probably recognise a few of those perceptions. Maybe, and most likely, you have a few others as well. And no matter what, everything is as it should be.

Because I completely believe that not only does everything happen for a reason, but that there is a gift in everything. I know that my soul has wished to experience this twisted love in order to transform them into a higher and more true expression of Love. I believe that the same goes for you and all souls that are incarnated on Earth in this time. One of the biggest tasks we all have right now is to make this transformation in our own personal lives.

In recent years, I have learned that the twists of love I absorbed in my childhood are much more widespread than I thought. For many years I was under the impression that they were very specific and personal experiences to me. Today, I know that they have been a natural part of life in 3D, and something that nearly everyone from my generation recognises in different ways. Because of that, it is my hope that the solutions and tools in this book to heal and transform the twists will resonate with you.

Maybe you are able to evolve out of the old love-programmes with a partner that you have lived with for many years. Maybe you have been experimenting with what is true Love for you in multiple relationships. Or maybe you may have chosen to let go of intimate relationships and might have had a long period of time where you are primarily close to yourself. No matter which way we each choose, we are all doing the same thing — we are upgrading our consciousness of Love from 3D to 5D.

So, let's get started with how you can get your personalised twisted love straightened out, so you can match your Love with the high-vibrational energy of 5D.

CHAPTER 2

Loving You

The Origin of Everything

As I mentioned earlier, the journey we are on in the paradigm shift is a journey where we are getting closer to our soul and true essence. Who we *truly* are. Who we have forgotten we are due to the dense veil that has separated life on Earth in 3D from the truth of ourselves. A journey where we reclaim ourselves. So, who is it we truly are?

To get closer to that, it is good to look closer at our origin. Our creator. Because as we as children here on Earth carry the essence of our parents' and ancestors' genes and patterns within us, our souls also carry the essence of the creator that birthed them. Whether we call that life-giving energy God, Allah, Chi, Prana, Source, Creator, or any other name, the essence of the source from which all of our souls are created is LOVE. I like to call my origin *Divine Love*; it resonates with a profound truth deep within me.

So far, so good.

If you accept my reasoning, then our true essence is Love because our creator is Love. That means that the reclamation of ourselves is the same as the reclamation of Love within ourselves. The more we establish a stable state of Love in our own way of being in the world, the closer we get to our origin and the closer we get to who we truly are. If we reject ourselves, we reject Love. If we reject Love, we reject our creator — and the origin for everything that is. From that point of view, it is actually quite a grave thing to *not* love ourselves if we want to evolve spiritually and get closer to a world where Love is the sustaining power. And if we want to be able to meet others with Love and spread more Love around us. It is impossible if we cannot first feel Love for ourselves.

The source that our Love needs to be nourished from is connected to our origin, the Divine Love, which fills our cup of Love from within our heart so we have something to give away. When we are truly loving humans, it isn't our personal Love we ooze off, but the universal Love that's always available to us all. And to open up for that source, we have to open up to Loving ourselves. That is the portal to the infinity source of Love. So, to judge yourself, criticise yourself, blame yourself, accuse yourself, hate yourself, be angry at yourself, and be merciless to yourself — that's pure poison if you want to open up to your inner source of Love. You have probably heard the saying: *You can't give to others what you cannot give yourself,* and that is as true as can be. If you can't or won't open up to loving yourself, you are closing off the source which can provide you with the Love you can pass on to others.

This makes me want to mention Anita Moorjani again, who has been a huge source of inspiration in my process of rediscovering Love. Anita is an author and a teacher, and today she travels across the globe to spread the word about how important it is that we humans learn to love ourselves. What brought her on that path was her very serious course with stage four cancer, a course through which she died and left her body, in what we call a near-death experience. During this near-death experience, she encountered a series of realisations. Partly on why she had gotten sick, partly on why life on Earth is as it is, and partly on how she could heal herself if she returned to her earthly life. The answer to everything was, in short, about self-Love and the lack of it. In her first book, *Dying to Be Me*, she describes how her stay in the spirit world gifted her with the realisation that the Love we are able to offer to others is a "side-effect", so to speak, of the appreciation and compassion we feel for ourselves as the magnificent creatures we truly are. In her teachings Anita emphasises that the common perception of self-Love and selfcare as being the root of destructive selfishness is a total falsehood. What she learned from her near-death experience was the opposite:

"Selfishness comes from too little self-Love, not too much, as we compensate for our lack."

Anita concludes that if we all cared about ourselves more, most of the judgment, insecurity, fear and mistrust that rules our world would disappear.

(You can find a list of the authors and books I mention at the back of this book.)

It is a message that is not to be mistaken. I sincerely recommend Anita's books and videos if you are looking for more perspective on why the ability to love yourself is so incredibly essential to the process of creating a new and more loving world.

I hope you are with me so far in concluding that strengthening the Love for yourself is the key to unlocking the Love vibration inside you. It is that which makes Love live, breathe, and pulsate within you, so you can feel that you ARE Love, and thus give Love to others so they too can experience that they ARE Love.

Another one of the world's prominent self-Love teachers is Louise Hay, who, in her 2018 book *Trust Life*, explains it this way:

"I find that when we really love and accept and approve of ourselves exactly as we are, then everything in life works."

What Louise is pointing out is that when self-Love becomes the foundation for your way of life, a natural flow will occur that makes everything in your life easier. It won't necessarily be a problem-free, happy-go-lucky life, but a life where you can get back on track much quicker when you experience challenges and stagnation. A life where the basis of your existence is trust, optimism, and satisfaction. These are all states of being that naturally follow when you and your life are founded in a deep Love for yourself.

From this state, you will open your arms to life's challenges with curiosity because you have the capacity and trust that they will do you good. The fear of what accidents the challenges may bring doesn't get a hold of you since Love and fear quite simply cannot exist in your system simultaneously; they are opposed on a vibrational level. When fear can't take hold of you, your creation

*when you learn
to love yourself,
everything in
your life works*

process comes from a higher vibrational level where what you attract and create also vibrates higher. This also goes for your inner state and experiences. You are moving from what I call *the little self's (the ego's) circle of creation* to *your higher self's spiral of creation* — a movement up the vibrational ladder that we are all in the middle of taking on in our own unique way on this transition from 3D to 5D. Much more on this in Chapter 5.

Such a high vibrating life is also what Abraham-Hicks in their teaching material *Co-Creating at Its Best* call life on "the high-flying disc". From this, we can begin to build a new world together, where we see the Divine Love in ourselves and each other, and where Love is the sustaining power in our shared work of creation. That is what a life founded in a deep Love within ourselves has in store for us. But if that's the truth about us, about Love, and about life — and if this new 5D energy wants us to open our eyes to it — how is it that it has been so difficult for us to understand this while we were in 3D? Why is the interconnectedness between loving ourselves and loving others so foreign to us? Why have we complicated this simple key *to make everything in life work,* as Louise Hay says, to the extent that we have in the old energy?

It is, of course, because we have ingrained these imprints of twisted love that life in 3D has consisted of on our subconscious mind, which has created a myriad of misconceptions. This has drawn us far away from the simple, profound, enlightening truths. Precisely as it was meant to be, because we had to forget who we were to rediscover ourselves on a deeper level when the time came. This has been the soul's intention all along, and now the time has come here at the doorstep to 5D. Before we continue with our journey of reclamation and rediscovery, let's take a look at one of the biggest misconceptions of Love in 3D.

Self-Centredness vs. Self-Love

One of the 3D twists that has had the most significant impact on our way of practising Love is the one that says that to love oneself is the same as self-centredness. It is a belief that the Christian church especially has helped cement. Luther warned against appreciating oneself too much and used the phrase *to be curved inward on oneself* (incurvatus in se) — which he believed led to egotism and unhealthy self-centredness. This warning against loving oneself has persisted within Christian culture to this day and has had an enormous influence on our way of understanding — and misunderstanding — Love.

One of the things I hear most often when I do courses, lectures, and coaching on self-Love is precisely this fear of being selfish. *"Now, it shouldn't be all about me"* is one of the most common phrases I hear when I encourage people to start strengthening their Love for themselves. There is a widespread fear that everything will spill into egotism and narcissism when we begin to meet ourselves with more Love and empathy. A fear that I am certainly familiar with from my own process. This fear has had especially fertile conditions in the previously mentioned new age circles which have held the energy for the new Love-based approach to life and humanity since the 1970s. As I mentioned, this group consisted primarily of women. And since women in our patriarchal society by definition are even less allowed to appear egotistical and selfish, the fear of being *curved inward on oneself* has dominated these circles.

This has meant that the Love new age women in the first years practised and presented, was a kind of sacrificial and self-destructive Love with a large focus on other people's needs, desires, and wellbeing. Whereas, to take care of one's own needs, desires, and wellbeing has been much less common. The philosophy of life that has dominated the new age world — which is based on the first sprouts of the 5D mindset — has been full of mantras right up the alley of the 3D-woman's perception of Love. That is to say, the sacrificial and self-ignoring love.

Let me share a couple of examples from my own life, so you know what I am talking about.

When I have listened to spiritual messages from various spiritual guides throughout the years, the term *unconditional Love* has, time and time again, come up in their messages. For many years, I thought this meant I should love other people unconditionally, despite their actions. I thought that it meant I had to choose to look at the positive, just like *God only sees the good in all of his children*. It didn't occur to me that this practice of unconditional Love also applied to me. And it definitely didn't occur to me that it first and foremost applies to me and *then* others. That I had to take good and loving care of my own boundaries and protect my own energy, before I practised empathy and Love for others. That way of understanding unconditional Love was a foreign concept to me which both societal norms and my own childhood trauma, of course, played their own part in supporting.

So, when I heard the words *unconditional Love*, I only understood it as something that should be directed towards others. And I strongly suspect that the same applies to many women from my generation — especially the holistic and alternative ones who, from all of their heart, wished to spread a Love-based energy around them. This has created a lot of burnout and exhaustion amongst these women.

Another example:

Throughout the years when I heard of another growing 5D-concept about how *we are all connected, which means that what I send out has an impact on everyone* — the same happened, just the opposite way around. I took on way too much responsibility for what I sent out, to the point where I basically took on the responsibility for nearly *everything* that was happening around me. I didn't even think to expect that other people were doing the same, and I certainly didn't think to set any clear and healthy boundaries for myself so that other energies couldn't morph with mine without reflection. I became the boundless and over-responsible woman who took on guilt and let others invade me. This was, of course, also supported by the societal and personal twisted love.

So, the interpretation Christian churches have of Jesus' words, *"You shall love your neighbour as yourself"* — where the last two words *"as yourself"* have slipped away and the mantra in our culture has been reduced to *"love your neighbour"* — has snuck its way into all the nooks and crannies of my, and I dare say, yours and all of our fellow humans' consciousness'. Especially women's. The interpretation permeates through us so much that we have twisted the words of wisdom on *unconditional Love* in a way where they mysteriously do not apply to ourselves.

It is one of the most significant and worst twists of love that ever happened in 3D. And, because of that, it is the twist that we need to undo the most as we get ready to begin our life in 5D. We do this by simply starting to strengthen our self-Love. How we do that, we will get to soon. But before that, let's take a look at the mechanisms the ego has performed for centuries so you can recognise them in yourself when they appear. Trust me, they will emerge once you seriously start to strengthen your Love for yourself. The ego isn't very interested in that. Not because it is evil, or stupid, or doesn't wish you any good, but because it's simply scared of change. The ego lives by the mantra: *You know what you have, not what you will get.* It does all it can to uphold the status quo, so you don't get into deep water. At its core, the ego's positive intention is to protect you from situations where you are not in control. The better you know this intention and the mechanism that belongs to it, the better you can calm your ego down and avoid its attempts at preventing you from expanding your self-Love.

You and your higher self know better. You know that strengthening your ability to love yourself opens doors for so many possibilities to create a new and more blissful life, than what the ego's strategies have ever been able to do. Even though the road ahead entails the unpredictable and uncontrollable. Let's take a closer look at our dear ego's fundamental mechanisms.

The Ego's Judgement

Life in 3D, and thus the ego's foundation, is first and foremost anchored in dualism. That is to say, the belief that everything is divided into opposites: Good-bad, loving-evil, intelligent-unintelligent, dark-light, etc. We have a wealth of these polarisations that we are taught to divide everything into. This also applies to other people, things that happen, and it applies to ourselves. This means that an important trait to have in the 3D world has been judging and assessing everything. To survive in 3D we have had to constantly decide whether what we experience is something to meet or run from. This goes all the way back to the classic collision with an animal in the savanna: Is it a gazelle or a tiger? Is it safe or dangerous? Does it mean life or death?

It has been a necessary reaction and still is as we move into 5D. To distinguish what is good for us and what isn't is an essential skill for our wellbeing. In that way, our taught dualistic judgement isn't something we should scold or distance ourselves from. Just like the twisted love and other patterns we have been given by previous generations is something that our souls have

*love your
neighbour as
yourself*

wanted to experience, to view the world through a dualistic lens is something we have chosen to go through to see where it takes us.

The way we have used our judgement in 3D is naturally based on the ego's consciousness and fundamental understanding, as that is what has dominated. You might recall from Chapter 1 that the ego's consciousness rests on the belief that we are separate from others, and that there isn't enough Love, room, and resources for us all to survive. This has meant that we have lived in a state of vigilance on the outside world. We have kept a constant eye out for the lurking dangers hiding in the shadows. We have lived in competition with other people and noted down if they are better, more beautiful, cleverer than us. Because if they were, that could be a threat to our existence. This is how dualistic judgement has infiltrated every part of our life in 3D.

It has caused our egos to develop a critical approach to everything and everyone, including ourselves. Life in 3D has certainly been built on finding mistakes, because focusing on mistakes and what's missing has been the most familiar and safe. It has, in many ways, stood in the way of a loving and empathetic approach, because we haven't balanced it with an accompanying focus on the resources and positive skill sets that are also at play. In ourselves, other people, and our lives. So, when you begin to train your self-Love muscle, and your Love-muscle in general, it is important to be aware that the ongoing judgemental, evaluating, and critical voice that surely will make itself heard every now and then, stems from a coping mechanism that was necessary back then, but not anymore in this western world.

It will *not* cost you your life to remove your awareness of the external circumstances and instead turn it towards the internal. It will *not* be dangerous to relax and let go of your vigilance to let yourself dwell in empathy for yourself. It will *not* rob you of your safety to let go of scepticism and suspicion, and instead start practicing open-mindedness and space for other people. You will *not* be burnt at the stake, hung, or exposed to public humiliation when you try to avoid judging and assessing everything about yourself, and when you stop keeping certain sides of yourself hidden. When you loosen up on self-criticism and blame, the world will *not* move ahead of you, and you will *not* risk being ostracised from the tribe and from society. And if you are, you can now, contrary to previous times, join new communities that match you and your essence more than the ones that reject you.

The only thing you risk by stopping the autopilot judgement and criticism of yourself and others is to create a more calm, thoughtful, and empathetic way to be in the world. It isn't as dangerous as we think. Or as your ego — your little self — thinks. You have a larger part of yourself — your *higher self* — that's both wiser and more loving. It is that part you have to rediscover when you read the following sections and chapters about how you can embrace a deeper and more unconditional Love for yourself. It is that part that's going to be the captain of this journey you are about to embark on. It is that part of you that's going to take the hand of your ego/little self, calm it down, and assure it that the journey you have set out on will bring you to a much better place than what the little self could possibly imagine. And assures that you will take care of your little self and make sure that everything happens at a pace you can all follow. That higher part of you will tell your little self that there is a new time and a new life that's standing ahead of you — a life where clinging to judgement, evaluation, and criticism will only create more pain and loss of life. Loss of Love. Loss of happiness. Loss of passion. Loss of excitement. Loss of meaning. Loss of satisfaction. Loss of …

It is that part — your higher, wiser, more loving self — that is in much better touch with your soul and the truth of who you are that's now taking charge. As you might remember from Chapter 1, your higher self knows full well that the ego's belief of separation and various frightening scenarios are nothing but illusions. In reality, you are connected to all other people and your creator in one huge, loving, universal field. So, when you do something good for yourself, like meeting yourself in a more loving and empathetic way, it will do good for everyone else, too. The Love you are filled with will then automatically flow through to everyone you surround yourself with. Even the ones you don't surround yourself with. Because Love's flowing energy doesn't know about borders and is not limited by time, and space, and other 3D beliefs. Your efforts to strengthen your self-Love and heighten the vibrations in the shared human consciousness benefits everyone.

It is a genuine paradigm shift you must make in your consciousness. You need to commit to letting Love reign over fear. To let the soul reign over the ego. You need to decide that your way of being in the world from now on will be determined from the inside, where you can be peacefully and empathically navigated by your inner GPS. Instead of being driven by the fear of being erased, and thus navigating from what is happening in your surroundings. Let's take a look at how you create this shift. We will start off by reconnecting with your inner GPS through self-empathy.

Self-Empathy

Just as with unconditional Love, the same thing has happened to the term empathy, where it is primarily understood and practiced as a quality that we direct towards others and not ourselves. And that is, of course, the case because Love and empathy are inseparable from each other. I can't have a loving approach to myself or another human being without simultaneously having an empathetic approach. So, one of the most important ways we can begin strengthening our Love for ourselves is by strengthening our empathy for ourselves. We do this by starting to give ourselves permission to sense how we are *really* feeling. Life in 3D, and the twisted love that has followed, has for many of us meant that we have covered the most vulnerable place within with layer upon layer of protection. This means that we have pulled ourselves away from being able to tell how we actually *feel*. It has been a necessary and good mechanism in 3D which has helped us survive the rigid emotional climate 3D has offered us.

In recent years, many people are starting to wake up to the truth of how much we have packed away and closed off to survive 3D. There is a wave of wounded inner children appearing and pleading to be seen, listened to, and met. This is happening for people of my own age and older, the group who back in "the old days" calmed down, and enjoyed their grandchildren, and didn't expect much more evolvement. It is also happening to the younger generations. It seems like the dismissed and exiled vulnerable sides of us all, regardless of age, no longer can or want to live hidden away, as if they don't exist. This wave of awakening is a result of the vibrational rise on Earth. The higher the vibrations and the closer we get to 5D's frequency, the more transparency and transillumination will appear in all of the unconscious and darkness. We experience this in our own lives when the hidden children appear and insist on being healed. And we experience it in a collective sense when one skeleton after the other falls out of the closet and shows us what has been happening in the shadows of the low vibrations in the 3D world. Bank scandals, abuse of power, child abuse, deception and profit-mongering by big businesses, illegal surveillance, and corruption within old, well-revered organisations that we have trusted are only a few examples.

But back to self-empathy, which is a good place to start when you want to strengthen the Love for yourself. But how do you do it?

Your Inner GPS

Let's begin by looking at what empathy is. At its core, empathy lets you stand in someone's shoes. To feel, acknowledge, and understand how the person is feeling and what they need. When we are speaking about self-empathy, it is about establishing an empathetic connection with yourself to feel how you were/are doing in certain situations, past or present. Maybe you need to establish an empathetic connection with your inner child, or with the person you were (or are) in certain situations, where you were/are harassed and harmed, or where your emotional reactions were/are set aside by yourself or others.

Empathy is, first and foremost, about connecting with *feelings*. Were/are you sad, scared, angry, disappointed, shocked — these are just a few questions you can ask yourself about your emotional state to determine whether there might be something important you needed/need. This is an important thing to remember about our emotional reactions — they always come with an important message for us about our *needs*. Either they are telling us that something important is missing or something important is present in our lives. I learned about this connection between feelings and needs many years ago from Marshall Rosenberg, the founder of *Nonviolent Communication* (NVC), which is also referred to as *empathetic communication*. When I learned that and began to adopt it, it made a defining difference to my communication, but also to my way of understanding and tackling my feelings — and thus my life altogether.

In NVC, we use the insight about our feelings and needs that we gain from the self-empathetic process to communicate more authentically, more clearly, and non-violently with others. But you can also use the insight to communicate more authentically, more clearly, and non-violently with yourself. It is the self-empathetic process that gives you a deeper understanding of yourself and your reactions in different situations. Through this, you will gain the ability to make decisions and choices that benefit and meet your important needs, so you can improve your well-being.

But how do you do that?

Firstly, by anchoring this wisdom in your system. When you experience feelings in the *uncomfortable* category like the ones I have mentioned before, then they will tell you that there is something that you are missing. The need you have was/is *not* met in the situation, and you have to address this need to feel good again. So, the uncomfortable feelings are a type of *you-have-to-change-direction* message from within. It is the opposite if you experience feelings in the *comfortable* category — e.g., happiness, excitement, peace, trust, satisfaction, and many others — as they come with the important message of how what you are experiencing right now is really good for you because your needs *are* met. So, the comfortable feelings are a type of *keep-on-doing-what-you-are-doing* message from within.

In that sense, you can think of your emotional system as your inner GPS, as I like to call it. It is a very fine navigational system that we all are born with, and which is designed to guide us in life so we thrive, grow, and have a good time. You could say that it's the soul's compass. The challenge is that we — just like with self-Love — pretty early on in our 3D lives have had our access to the navigational system, which builds on self-empathy, disturbed or even completely cut off. We are taught to go to our head and think, rationalise, and explain away our feelings instead of using them as the important messengers of our needs that they really are. When you want to strengthen your self-empathy and reconnect with your inner GPS, it's really about starting to focus on the needs that hide behind your feelings. We can say that it's like going to your body/heart instead of your head/brain. It makes a vast difference in the way you experience your feelings and the duration the uncomfortable feelings are allowed to take hold of you for. Because when you recognise the needs behind the feeling and act in a way that meets those needs, it changes the uncomfortable feeling to comfortable. Its mission has been accomplished, the message is understood, and there is no longer a need for it.

Throughout your life if you have put many layers of protection over the softest place within — thus drifting further away from the connection with what is actually happening in your emotional cave — you might need to

*your inner
GPS is a
compass of
the soul*

go through the inner GPS process in stages. You might need a period to concentrate just on feeling your feelings. This is to say to let yourself register how you are feeling without having to focus too much on finding and defining the needs behind it. But when you have gotten better at being in touch with your feelings, it is important that you move on and begin to tune in to the needs that lie behind them. It is here the magic of self-empathy lies. It is here transformations happen. It is here where the GPS-lady — in the shape of the uncomfortable feelings — goes quiet and changes into the peace and calmness of the daisy path.

Because when you, through self-empathy, discover that you are sad *because* your need to be heard was/is not met, you can start to do something about it — e.g., by asking the person who isn't listening to you to sit down and start doing so. Or by starting to listen to yourself if that person is no longer in your life. Or by removing yourself from people who do not listen to you, no matter how many times you have asked them to.

And when you, through self-empathy, discover that you are frustrated *because* your need for a deep connection and presence with your partner is not met, you focus on that need. You can work on creating situations that fit the need for a more present-minded connection. Or you can ask your partner to watch less television or be more at home. Or even consider if you should leave the relationship because you realise that your need for presence and deep connection will never be met in that relationship.

And when you, through self-empathy, discover that you are angry *because* your need to trust a person has been let down, you can communicate it in a more constructive way. You can tell the person that you are angry because you need to be able to trust them, and then find a path together that ensures such a letdown won't happen again. Or you can communicate with yourself — is it realistic that such a betrayal of trust won't happen again, and if it does can you live with that? Or should you remove yourself from the situation to take care of your needs and spare yourself further betrayal?

I hope you can see how the self-empathetic process, where you search for the needs behind your feelings, moves you from paralysation and the feeling of being at the mercy of your emotions, to being able to actively handle the situations where you experience those uncomfortable feelings. We often feel powerless when difficult and uncomfortable feelings take charge of us. But when we begin to understand that they always come with an important message to us about our unfulfilled needs, we remove ourselves from that powerlessness and move towards proactivity.

That is why it is so incredibly important that you do not let yourself stay in a state where you feel your difficult emotions, but are not aware of what it is they want to tell you. To be swimming in uncomfortable and difficult emotions for a long time rarely does anyone any good, and it is not a particularly self-loving act. Self-Love, on the other hand, is to take your feelings seriously, welcome them, and ask what it is they want to tell you, fully knowing that they, of course, are there for a good reason and with an important message. A self-loving act is also to remember to honour and respect your feelings by frequently thanking them for the messages they bring you to help you thrive and flourish. At the end of this chapter, there is an exercise to help you practise this.

From the Ego's Mindset to the Soul's Mindset

To get the inner GPS to function frictionlessly and automatically, as it was designed by our creator and as it did when we were small kids, requires time and training for most of us. This is due to the same reasons I talked about at the beginning of this chapter — regarding the difficulties of practising unconditional Love towards ourselves. Unconditional Love and self-empathy are, as mentioned, inseparable from one another; they are two sides of the same coin.

In the ego's mindset, which we are taught in our 3D life, it is a foreign concept that I should be worthy of being loved unconditionally — regardless of my behaviour and performance, but simply because I am me and I am here. And it is a foreign way of thinking that I, in all of life's situations — even when I am filled with difficult and "ugly" feelings — should be worthy of being met with empathy and interest, and not judgement and assessment. But in the mindset of the soul, it is self-evident to love and show compassion in all situations. Because the soul knows that there is *always* a good reason that you are reacting the way you do, even when you are filled with "ugly" emotions and are reacting "unreasonably" and "irrationally". The soul has a deep understanding and respect for your motives, your feelings, your needs, and your behaviour patterns. It loves you unconditionally and always comes from an empathetic perspective, regardless of how you behave. Its most sincere wish is that you, as a physical human being, will begin to understand *how* loved you are, and *how* amazing you are, and *how* valuable and significant your life is.

Let's end this section about self-empathy by cementing that there are, of course, situations in life where you are filled with strong and difficult feelings that you, at first glance, can't transform, despite identifying the hidden need. That may, i.e., be if you are scared or sad because you are given a serious diagnosis, or if you are grieving because you have lost someone close. In situations like those, it can be difficult to change the situation and the feelings by actively taking charge. Here, you can meet yourself with empathy by giving the emotions permission to be there, and to do what they need to do without beating yourself up with the illusion of moving on or reacting in a certain way. The most self-empathetic thing to do in the harshest moments of life is often to allow ourselves to be and feel exactly as we are — without judgement, criticism, or blame.

But even in those situations, the method I have given you in this section can often still be useful. Because sometimes the worst part of a situation where you have lost someone close is not that they are no longer here, but that you and your surroundings have different takes on how you should react. By searching behind the feeling, you might find the need to be allowed to be exactly who you are and to react exactly as you do. And if that's what you come up with, you can actually be proactive by asking well-meaning people to just be there and not say anything about what they think you should do. On the other hand, if you find out that your need is to be completely alone with your grief and loss, you can take care of that by telling the people around you that you are spending a week or two by yourself at a grief-retreat. So even if what lies around your difficult emotions does not immediately change, you can use the process of self-empathy and your inner GPS to handle the situation in a self-loving and self-empathetic way, which makes the situation easier to bear. This might also mean that you will get through the grief in a more graceful and constructive way.

Meet Everything with Love

Beyond self-empathy, there exists another, just as important, way of strengthening your love for yourself. This is also a way that neutralises the ego's autopilot which wants to judge and criticise. And while the autopilot, for most of us, is fastened thoroughly to the seat, there is a need for more than just one type of medicine to neutralise it once you decide that you are going to strengthen your self-Love.

This other medicine is inspired by Matt Kahn and is called *Meet Everything with Love*. And when it says *everything*, it means *everything*. Both what happens within you and how you are reacting, and what happens within others and how they are reacting. But for the time being, as you are reclaiming your self-Love, let's keep it to *everything that happens within you and your reactions*. It is good to make a, perhaps long-term, stop at this point to fight against the autopilot's tendency to start practising *meeting everything everyone else is doing* with Love. Because, as you know, many of us have a tendency to think that unconditional Love is more so about others than ourselves. And we now know that's a big misconception and it is in fact the other way around. We, first and foremost, have to learn to meet *ourselves* with unconditional Love, and then let the Love we generate in our hearts flow through to others. Thus giving from a full cup, not a half-empty one — in that way there is more Love for everyone. So right now, it is called *meet everything that happens within you with Love*. And what does that mean? How do you do it?

What happens within you is partly those feelings and needs we touched on regarding self-empathy. But it is also, i.e., thoughts, physical sensations, different impulses towards actions, and regular actions. But regardless of what it is, you meet it with Love. You can do this by honouring and meeting your feelings and being interested in the needs behind them, as we talked about earlier. But you can also do this by meeting your, perhaps negative or frightened, thoughts with empathy. Instead of automatically falling into the ego's judgemental and condemning trap where you think to yourself: *"It is cruel of me to think about him like that."* Or: *"I should think differently."* Or: *"Come*

*meet
everything
that happens
within you
with love*

on, *why am I so scared? It doesn't make any sense."* Or perhaps the worst kind: *"Oh no, I just thought negatively again, so I am probably attracting something negative."* Instead, you practice meeting your thoughts with compassion and interest.

It may sound like this in your head: *"What need could it be that I am not meeting in my relationship with him since I think about him this way?"* Or: *"What is it the little girl/boy within me needs since she/he was so scared in this situation?"* Or: *"What might it be that makes me think negatively about this? Is it a part of me that doesn't like what is happening? A part of me I have lost touch with?"* Do you see how this is a different way of meeting yourself? The soul's way. Your clever and loving soul who knows that there is always a good reason for you to think, feel, and act the way you do; and who is interested in that reason so you can face what is at play and return to the daisy path.

You can show the same compassionate interest for physical sensations like pain and tension that, perhaps repeatedly, is happening and annoys you. The soul's way of approaching them is with an equally loving interest to what type of message the body is presenting. The body always wants to guide you to a life with more wellness. And it is when you aren't listening that it needs to speak up. So, listen to your body and what it's trying to tell you with compassionate curiosity. It might sound like this in your head: *"What do you need me to do, dear beloved body, so that you can get better? What is it that you want me to know? How can I best listen, dear body, and understand the message you are bringing to me?"*

When you ask those types of questions, you might not get answers right away. But be vigilant and observant with what comes to you after you have asked. This can be in the shape of answers and realisations from within, through your dreams, through messages from other people, songs, or something you hear and see on TV, on the radio, in books, etc. The Divine Love speaks in many ways.

You can also focus the soul's loving approach towards impulses and actions you actually want to put an end to. This can be bad habits or addictive behaviour that you want to change. These types have never listened to, let alone adjusted themselves to, the criticising and judgemental voices that you have probably attempted to use uncountable times. It just does not work. But a compassionate curiosity for what lies behind the behaviour or habit will open up a different and more productive dialogue with the part of yourself that runs it. This is again from a trust that there is, of course, a good reason that one part of you wants something, while another part of you wants to stop. When you engage in a loving and empathetic dialogue with those two parts of you, you have a much better chance of modifying your behaviour in a way that serves you well. When we speak of addiction, it is very often the case that our inner child was frozen at a point in time where life was too difficult to bear. The addictive behaviour, whether it is abuse of alcohol, food, shopping, work, or something else, provides a numbing effect so that you can't feel the pain. To get closer to your inner child, who is hiding behind the addictive behaviour, with Love and empathy is a much better strategy than control and restrictions. Because Love will dissolve the pain that provides fuel to the addiction. You can do this by asking yourself questions like the ones from the previous examples, and you can use the loving mantras that I suggest in the Exercises & Tips section at the end of this chapter.

MY QUEST FOR RECLAMATION — AND YOURS

My process of reclaiming Love has taken place through several cycles. Many years ago, I, for the first time, became aware of the vitally important role of self-Love in my journey back to my essence. I have always listened to messages from the spiritual world delivered to people on Earth through various mediums. A part of me has known that these messages held truths that could be difficult for those of us in the physical dimension to get in touch with. Truths that we need to know to further evolve.

One of those truths has been about learning to love ourselves. About how important it is that we exercise an understanding of how loved and valued we are, and how we need to stop criticising ourselves, and instead start looking at ourselves with kinder and more compassionate eyes. That wisdom has been essential for me on this journey to "give myself permission" to continue focusing on my self-Love. Over and over again. I have gone through many cycles in this process where I, each time, have reclaimed a small part of true Love for myself. I have several times thought that *now* I have finally learned it, only to discover a new aspect of my behaviour I could focus on and dig even deeper into.

In the recent years, on par with the still rising vibrational energy that's surging towards Earth, I, like many others, have acquired tools and methods that cut even deeper into what true self-Love is. And what true Love even is. I have moved from applying more Love to the way I treat myself in my everyday life, to changing my very way of being in the world. In a way, it is a movement from the outside-in — from external behaviour patterns to an inner state of being. Over time, I have moved through countless veils and layers that I was taught when I was a child, and thus believed were natural and necessary twists of love. And as I have worked my way through them and gotten in touch with a deeper layer of true Love, there are again new veils and layers that need and want to be looked at.

In this process, *Al-Anon's Twelve Steps* have been one of the biggest gifts to see through my co-dependency patterns and bring more self-Love into my life. I have gone through numerous healing and therapy approaches over the past thirty years, but if I had to point to the one that's been the most beneficial, it would be the step-work. To go through one's life and behavioural patterns with a wise and compassionate sponsor in the way that the Twelve Steps programme sets it up is an incredibly liberating and self-loving act. It sheds so much light and clarity on the autopilot's destructive reaction patterns, that they simply can't live on and drain you of your energy. It has at least been like that for me, and I sincerely encourage you to test the work with those Twelve Steps if you need a new lens on your dysfunctional behavioural patterns. Search for Al-Anon, ACA, or AA in the area you live in and find a group you can meet up with. It is a free global network where any and all are welcome.

Some years ago, when I began the latest cycle of my self-Love process, I read the book *The Gift of Our Compulsions* by Mary O'Malley. In it, she described how her self-Love work led to how, when she passed by a mirror, she began to register a sense of Love bloom in her heart purely from the sight of herself. At that moment, I made it a goal that I wanted to get to that point. I found it incredibly beautiful, and read it as an important and meaningful step when the Love for myself could be felt in the heart and not "just" from my ability to take care of myself, treat myself, listen to myself, etc. Today, I want to say that I was right. It is a defining shift to arrive at a state in the heart where loving myself is something I can feel, and not something I exercise from the mind, or fight for my right to do. I would lie if I said that I constantly feel a profound state of Love every time I catch a glimpse of myself in the mirror. But I am encountering an exceedingly more positive and loving look at myself. And I often notice that I am giving totally spontaneous, encouraging statements to myself, i.e., in the form of compliments. Not because I include it as part of my training program of mirror work that I have been diligent with over the passing years — which you will get an exercise on soon — but as something that comes naturally from within, because treating myself positively and lovingly has become my new way of being.

In the summer of 2020, I discovered another sign that my self-Love had reached a defining shift. I was using a guided heart-meditation in which I was encouraged to think about a near and dear person that awakens the feeling of Love in your heart. In previous practises of that kind, I have thought of my daughters, grandchildren, and a beloved pet to open the heart. But this summer, I experienced that the quickest opening of the heart came from a picture of myself as a child. I had this picture on my shelf because I, yet again, worked on healing the little girl inside, and now realised that the mere sight of the little girl and the thought of her brought out a blooming sensation of Love in my heart.

That being said, I am sure if you ask me in a year or two or ten, I will say that I have reached even more nuances and depths with my experience of loving myself. Just to make it clear, I don't think of my journey as finished — but as an ongoing process that's always opening up to new dimensions. As I wrote earlier, I am sure that the miracles and the magic that Love has up its sleeve for us, as we discover how to open up for it, will reach way beyond the imaginations of our 3D consciousness. But even though it's that way, and even though it calls for a certain humility, I still believe that it's important to note and acknowledge the progress we register in our process. So, I encourage myself and you to give ourselves a clap on the shoulder when we realise that we have moved ourselves one more step away from the ego's self-criticism and blame, and instead towards the soul's unconditional Love.

Twists of Love I Have Undone

If I had to put a few words to the twisted love that I have worked to resolve on my quest for reclamation, then it is about feelings of:

- Being worthless
- Not being good enough
- Fear of standing out and being myself
- Not being pretty, slim, tall, young, charismatic enough …
- Guilt of taking up too much space
- Guilt of being different
- Fear of fiasco
- Fear of being shamed/made fun of
- Fear of saying no/setting boundaries
- Fear of expressing my power through my voice and singing
- Fear of success
- Fear of losing control
- Fear of being sensitive
- And so much more

I trust that you recognise at least some of these patterns, because I know that they are very common twists of love in 3D. I have my own personal trauma from my childhood, as you read an example of in Chapter 1, and you have yours. But besides that, there have been so many collective and societal terms and conditions in our 3D life that have produced these emotional patterns. There aren't many who aren't familiar with them. Personally, I have uncovered them through the course of many years. In the beginning, they hid in the depths of the subconscious mind. I wasn't even aware that I had them, but I tried with all of my strength to survive, despite the disturbance they brought into my life. When I then began my quest for reclamation, and created more and more Love in my life, they ever so slowly began appearing, one after the other. Finally, there was space, compassion, and Love for them to be brave enough to show themselves.

I am sharing this so you are prepared if you have just ventured out on your own quest for reclamation and the same thing happens to you. Or if you are in the middle of your quest and are feeling that the emotional toll is just getting worse and worse. I want you to know that it is a completely natural and necessary part of the process for those hidden sides, our shadow sides, to appear from the fog and ask to be seen, heard, and met. When they do that, it can feel as if life just gets worse and worse. It can feel as if it was much better to just continue living within the bounds of our 3D consciousness — with all the blissful ignorance and denial that entails. And your ego will definitely attempt to convince you to stop what you are undertaking. The vulnerability and sensitivity that Love will reveal when we begin to open up to it can feel very scary.

This is when you have to strap your higher self into the driver's seat. The wise part of you knows that, when you give Love and compassion to all those parts that live hidden away in the darkness of your subconsciousness, YOU and LIFE will reveal itself so wonderfully and majestically that your little self can't even begin to imagine it. The wise part of you knows that it isn't even a possibility to avoid unlocking Love, because that's what our very life on Earth at this time is about, and that is, quite simply, why you have arrived in the first place. The wise part of you also knows that life in 3D is done, and if you keep holding onto your 3D perceptions, it will only create more pain and suffering. 5D has arrived and the best thing you can do for yourself is to follow the energy, say YES to the Love it has to offer, and liberate yourself from the untrue, twisted love that has been hiding your true, incredible, and unique essence.

The quest to reclaim Love for yourself will most definitely not be a journey that follows a straight path towards the goal. There will be resistance, challenges, obstacles, and regression throughout — and new parts of yourself will emerge that you initially won't like and will feel uneasy with. The key is to meet it all from the heart — not the brain who wants to judge, evaluate, and dispute everything that doesn't fit into the little self's belief of what you and your self-image can manage to unveil and acknowledge.

The best mantra you can support yourself with on this journey is then this: *Meet everything with Love and empathy*. In the following, you will receive three examples of how you can firmly adopt this mantra into your everyday life.

EXERCISES & TIPS

The following three exercises and tips on strengthening the Love and empathy for YOU are some of the ones I have used the most throughout my reclamation quest. They are inspired by three of the world's biggest teachers, whose wisdom I have gratefully implemented throughout my process: Louise Hay, Marshall Rosenberg, and Matt Kahn.

There is not anyone who has gone through their childhood and a good chunk of an adult life in 3D that doesn't have any emotional trauma of sorts. Exactly as our souls planned, so they could evolve — as you will recall. One of the ways we evolve is by becoming the loving and empathetic parent to ourselves that our earthbound parents were unable to be due to their trauma.

Each of these exercises are strong tools to nurture self-Love and self-empathy, which I encourage you to make part of your everyday life and your autopilot's way of meeting yourself.

EXERCISE 1
Mirror Work

Mirror work was presented to the world many, many years ago by self-Love's *wise old lady* Louise Hay. It is impossible to describe the impact her work and her many books, audio files, and card collections have had on humankind's awakening to a more loving approach to oneself, to life, and to each other. Furthermore, she also founded and developed Hay House — the world's biggest publishing company within spiritual self-development.

Louise Hay has given us a variety of effective tools to strengthen our self-Love, but according to herself in her last years of living, *mirror work* is still the most important one to follow. I have practised it in the following way and I encourage you to do the same.

This is how you do it:
During the day, every time I go to the bathroom and wash my hands, I look myself in the eyes in the mirror and say to myself, at least three or four times:

I love you, Ianneia.

I really love you.

You are an amazing being.

I hope you can feel how much I love you.

I recommend you do the same, using your own name, of course. Maybe you find some other phrases that suit you better. Let the phrases that come to your mind emerge and use them until you feel the urge to replace them with other phrases that hold more power. You can always go back to them again if they call on you. Over time, this practice is going to transform the way you look at yourself, if you keep doing it consistently.

And I am purposefully saying over time because it is consistency and repetition that makes the big difference. In her last years of living, as she was reaching ninety years old, Louise Hay said that she still did this every day and had been doing it for many, many years. Through this practice, she kept on discovering new dimensions of her self-Love.

But be prepared for resistance; the uncomfortable feelings and the critical and harsh voices that I mentioned earlier are guaranteed to emerge and try to provoke you. You might be experiencing grief and sadness when you begin talking to yourself this way. It is all completely natural parts of the process. You just have to keep going. Meet the uncomfortable, the resistance, the criticism, the grief, and the sadness with Love and persistence. Keep confirming that you mean it. You love yourself and you know that you are an amazing being that your creator loves beyond your imagination. Regardless of what will appear, you just keep going. You know that the resistance is only part of the 3D programming that is not in alignment with the truth — about You and about Life.

I promise that it will make a defining difference in your life. It has for me and millions of people across the globe. When we confront ourselves directly in the mirror and send a continuous stream of Love, we will one by one dissolve the outdated self-hatred, insecurity, self-criticism, worthlessness, etc. All of 3D's twisted love will be loved away, regardless of how they appear in our system.

EXERCISE 2

Send Love and Acceptance to Your Inner Children

This exercise is inspired by Matt Kahn, one of the younger contemporary self-Love teachers. In his book *Whatever Arises, Love That,* he encourages us to begin our own private *Love Revolution* by meeting every part of ourselves with Love. His argument for this is that every feeling, thought, behaviour pattern, and personality trait we contain are representatives of our inner children that are asking to be seen, listened to, and loved.

When I read Matt Kahn's book it really resonated with me and the inner-child healing I had practised for many years. It added to my understanding of the "inappropriate" behaviour I registered in myself from time to time. I saw that the immature thoughts, feelings, behaviour patterns, and personality traits had helped me to conform with the crowd and survive at some point in my childhood where it was too difficult for me to be ME. And now these inner children that I had abandoned tried to get my attention in my adulthood to check if there was room for being ME now.

The only key to get inside and get back in touch with these inner children is Love. That's what they need to feel safe enough to step into the light, so we can integrate them and become whole and thrive again. *Reclaim our innocence*, as Matt Kahn calls it. It is the same as when we refer to returning to *our true essence, our true I, our light, our power,* or *who we really are.*

The following is how I have practised sending Love and acceptance to those inner children, so they feel safe to emerge from their hiding places in the dark. When they feel loved and accepted, they stop using destructive and "inappropriate" behaviour to get attention.

This is how you do it:

Despite what may emerge within you — feelings, thoughts, pain, tension, behaviour — you will meet it with the *I Love You* mantra. Say it as gently and compassionately as you would to a child that is struggling.

Say the mantra out loud or in your head to yourself several times. Imagine you press the "repeat" button in your mind, so the mantra is said over and over again. Remember that we always have thoughts in our mind. The more we decide to have loving thoughts, and the less we let the autopilot run the show with it's not-so-loving thoughts, the more we speed up our process of overwriting the judgemental 3D-approach towards ourselves with a more loving 5D-aligned approach. Just like the mirror-work without a mirror.

And just like in the mirror-work, replace the *I Love You* mantra with other mantras that emerge in you which activate a relief and make you feel really good. These are phrases that you maybe have longed to hear all your life from others, but now you give them to yourself. (I, for instance, have said, *"You haven't done anything wrong whatsoever"* to myself many, many times until my inner child believed it and began to relax.)

Last but not least: let your way of saying the loving mantras develop how they desire to. You might want to sing it, whisper it, yell it, laugh it, expand it to *I love, love, love, love, love you — You are so, so, so beautiful!* — or something entirely else. Just let it happen and go with the flow that appears.

Reflecting on the exercise

Regardless of what kind of emotions, thoughts, and behaviours arise — this also goes for the many shadow sides that I mentioned earlier which are guaranteed to appear throughout your quest — Love is what they need. Feel the gentleness, the compassion, the Love towards yourself soften your heart so it slowly opens up, melting, and is filled with the nourishing and life-giving Love vibration.

You can use this method when you, i.e., get mad, jealous, greedy, annoyed, controlling — and all the other "ugly" feelings that arise in you. They aren't to be judged but loved away. You can also use it when you feel sad, scared, insecure, confused, and any other equivalent emotion. Or you can use it when you are happy, excited, out of control, wild, or something like that.

You can use the method when you are trying to fall asleep, when you wake up, when you meditate, go for a walk, cycle, and in other similar instances. It is a really good idea to, under all circumstances, repeat the loving mantras to yourself many times throughout the day. So it becomes a type of underlying stream in your automated thought activity, replenishing your system with Love while you are busy doing other things.

EXERCISE 3

Meet Your Difficult Feelings with Self-Empathy

We have already spoken about self-empathy. As you may remember the most important point is that *there is always a need hiding behind every feeling*.

When you are filled with comfortable feelings — when you are i.e., happy, satisfied, excited, relieved, safe — then it's because some of your important needs are met. When you are filled with uncomfortable feelings — when you are i.e., sad, scared, angry, frustrated, insecure — then it's because some of your important needs *are not* being met. When the latter happens, you can change the uncomfortable feeling by sensing what type of need it is that's not being met and then take action to meet it. The feeling of being trapped in that feeling will then change.

In this exercise, I will guide you through the self-empathy process for when you are experiencing difficult feelings, so you can get a sense of what it can provide you with.

This is how you do it:

Phase 1: Introduction. Sit or lay down comfortably somewhere you won't be disturbed. Have a pen and paper nearby, in case you will need to write something down. Take three deep breaths where you inhale Love and lightness, and exhale tension and unease.

Phase 2: Tune in. Think about a situation where you are filled with one or several difficult feelings. It can be a situation that is continuously happening in your life, i.e., in relation to your work or a close relationship, or it can be a single situation right now and here or of the recent past that is bothering you.

Begin tuning into the feeling that is emerging within you as you think about the situation. Try to meet the feeling as openly as possible and sense the nature of it. Is it anger, frustration, grief, disappointment, shock, impatience …? Take a deep breath and open up so you really *feel* it in your body. If you want to, you can take loud, deep breaths through your mouth, which will open up a stronger connection to your body.

Phase 3: Respect and Acknowledgement. Now show respect and appreciation towards the feeling. Approach it as you would an honourable and welcome guest that is arriving to bring you an important message. You know that the feeling is here out of Love for you. It is your trusty GPS-lady who is here to tell you something important about the path you are on. She wants to help you so you will avoid continuing down the wrong path.

Phase 4: Self-empathy. You are now showing interest in the message the feeling is bringing. Centre your awareness on the heart and ask: *"What is it you want to make me aware of? Which of my unmet needs do you want to tell me about?"* Or it might suit you more to talk directly to yourself instead of the feeling: *"What is it I need that I am not getting in this situation? What need is behind this feeling?"* Try to keep your attention on the heart and body so that you don't end up in the brain and begin to over-analyse. You are only interested in the message of what unmet need the feeling wants to make you aware of — not analysing the situation, you, or other people.

When you have spoken with your feeling and listened to its answer, you slowly exit the situation. This phase should not go on for more than one to two minutes. Anything more than that will risk you starting to overthink and interpret, instead of sensing in your heart which feelings and needs are at play. If you don't get an answer during the exercise, then be conscious of what comes to you throughout the day, in your dreams at night, when you wake up in the morning, and other ways. The answer will come, the key is to realise it when it is here. When you receive an answer about your unmet need, whether it is right away or later, you move onto Phase 5.

Phase 5: Self-care. When you know which need is not being met in the situation you tuned in on, you can start taking care of your need by thinking proactively.

- What can you do to meet the need?
- What can you ask others to do?
- Are there big or small changes regarding the situation, or regarding your life, that will ensure the need is met?
- Will/can you make these changes?
- How?

This is where you might need that pen and paper if a lot of ideas on how to tackle the situation in a way that satisfies your need are coming forth. Over the next hours/days, you can decide on which suggested actions you will carry into your life, and how, and when.

Reflecting on the exercise

Even if you aren't able to change the situation right here and now, it will always bring more ease to your system when you meet and honour your feelings and show interest in the needs behind. Just the way a sad child will calm down once an adult sees the child and tries to put words to their feelings and needs — *are you upset because you wanted to play with Emma?* — even if the need cannot be met.

Your system quiets down in the same way when your feelings and needs are seen and heard. That is the most important part of the empathetic process. If you can act on the insight as well, so you can change the situation that activates this feeling in the future, then that's an extra win which means your uncomfortable feeling will change.

With this exercise, you will show your system that you are a loving and compassionate parent to yourself. A parent who listens to you and takes you seriously, even when you are filled with the difficult "ugly" and "unreasonable" feelings. A parent who knows that there, of course, is a good reason for you to react the way you do — and who wants to help you get in touch with that reason. It is a very strong empathetic signal to send to yourself and your inner children, who without doubt will begin to have the courage to step out-side their hiding spots the more you show them that their needs are welcome and that you are there for them.

Be True to Yourself

Honour Your Unique Energy Signature

I am almost sure that you, throughout recent years, have heard the phrases *stand strong in your light, stand strong in yourself, move home into yourself* or maybe *be true to yourself* — which is the title of this chapter. These are all expressions that, in this paradigm shift, have spread far and wide within the self-development world. They all relatively mean the same thing, which is that the time has come for each and every one of us to stand strong as the person we truly are within, in ardent and authentic touch with our unique essence and the unique gift we have come to give to the world. Even though we all are connected through the big, interconnected, universal field, and we in that way are not separate (as the ego believes), we also each have our very own unique energy signature that no one else in the universe has. It can sound like a paradox; that we, at the same time, are inseparably connected and distinctively different. But that is one of the — to the ego — paradoxical truths that we have to begin absorbing and understanding in this transition to 5D.

I once read the book *Beyond Past Lives* by Mira Kelley, where she talks about a regression session she had with the spiritual teacher Wayne Dyer's daughter, Serena. In it, Serena is brought back to the place in the universe where souls are created and where she at one point in time worked. It is one of the most beautiful and touching descriptions I have ever read or heard of how we are each created. Serena describes how the creator sensed a void or an imbalance in the total energy field and then created a very specific combination of energies to fill and balance out that void. This very unique energy-signature was put into a soul with the mission to embody it and carry it out into the world. Thus, even before our soul was created, we have been wanted, treasured and loved. She also describes how the souls who are doing evil things and hurting others are very much treasured — and considered the bravest ones by the creator, since the dark energies are as much needed as the light for the evolution of the world and the souls.

What this regression shows us is that every soul contains a unique set of energies which the world needs. It is carefully decided how each of the energies in us will play together and how they are balanced. Only when the perfect energy combination has been completed can the soul go on and influence the world with its unique signature. This description gave me a profound under-standing of what is meant by: we are all unique, priceless creatures and we can't even begin to under-stand how appreciated we are by our creator — a message I have heard in different versions time and time again from the spiritual side. Serena's description put this message into a new context, and many things around my own and other's entitlement to be where we are, to be exactly who we are, and to do exactly as we do made sense. Personally, I realised that all of which I encompass — both what I weigh as good sides and bad sides — is a meaningful and valuable part of what my creator has put me in this world to share. It was obviously a solid boost to my ability to love and appreciate myself, and at the same time a good remedy against self-criticism and self-blame. The old mantra *All is Well* had a new meaning and depth. And my feeling of being loved and appreciated by The Divine was strengthened.

An important part of getting ready for life in 5D is that we learn to appreciate the unique energy signature we each carry within us. It is that which the many expressions at the beginning of this chapter covers. We are no longer supposed to show the world these half-hearted and clouded versions of our light and our power as we have done in 3D, where compromises and adjustments were a necessary condition of life. In 5D we begin to understand that it's an advantage that we are all unique, and that following our inner guidance instead of the herd is actually the best way we can give our unique gifts to the world. Whereas, in the 3D world, there have been some pretty strict limits on how much we could separate ourselves from societal norms without being deemed "abnormal" and "deviants". We are about to get used to a society where there is much more space to be different. A much more colourful and pluralistic society, you could say.

My old master Khutumi-Agrippa, from one of the mystery schools I attended throughout the years, once said, *"Do what you want — but harm no one."* That expression says it all. We are approaching a world where we each follow our own inner guidance, even if it goes against 3D's logic and rationale. At the same time, we are mindful of others and we don't harm anyone in our way. Which, by the way, becomes more and more unlikely, because when we are filled with high vibrations — that first of all are created through loving ourselves as we touched on in Chapter 2 — hurting anyone or anything becomes a very foreign concept. We are about to enter a society where the compassion that grows from our increased self-Love focuses the individual's behaviour towards a more loving and responsible direction. We can call it a society that's steered from an inner source rather than an outside source. That's why so many people in these years have a focus on their inner light and on liberating and unveiling their true essence. It comes as a necessity from within as the new energy settles in us.

Dependency

Before we get to how we help ourselves create our inner-steered voyage, let's take a look at the patterns that have prevented us from being true to ourselves and our own light in 3D. Then we will know what patterns we don't want to bring with us into our lives and relationships in 5D.

One of the overarching twists of love that have been normal in 3D is the confusion between dependency and Love. This twist has had an unbelievably significant influence on close relationships for centuries and probably millennia. Just looking at the past one hundred year love story that I described in Chapter 1, it is obvious that life in impoverished circumstances — which my grand-

*do what
you want -
but harm
no-one*

parents and partly my parents grew up in — naturally bred a dependent relationship between parties in romantic and family relations. When most of the time awake is spent making sure there is food on the table, the relationship between both man and woman, and parent and child, is inherently influenced by a sort of natural dependency on one another. So, to ask oneself, *"What is it that I really want, at my core?"* Or: *"What is the most profound essence of what my soul has come to give?"* — was a luxury most couldn't indulge. You entered working communities that were about survival and getting things to work. That does not mean that there couldn't be a deep and real Love in those relations — or that these types of relationships weren't both meaningful and satisfactory. But I have no doubt that the dependency that existed between the participants implied that Love in different ways had to be twisted. In each individual, compromises and adjustments to put your inner voice aside for the benefit of the group had to happen. This is again exactly as our souls wished for, so they could grow and evolve.

When my parents' generation became adults, the dependency of keeping the family together continued to be a condition for most, at least for the women. It wasn't until my generation, who were young in the '70s and '80s, that people achieved the economic freedom to take a stand on whether our closest relationships were satisfactory and had room for the kind of Love we desired. Our generation started a landslide of divorces in the wake of the youth revolt and women's liberation, which is still a phenomenon spread far and wide between all generations in our society. Today, almost everyone in our part of the world has the financial freedom to leave relationships where they don't thrive. Now that doesn't mean that patterns of dependency on the inner levels is a finished book. Just like the personal, emotional trauma that lives in the subconscious world long after the outer conditions change, dependency patterns also carry on living within us, despite us having our freedom. They reside deep within our subconscious and define our way of understanding and practising Love. In reality, the two parts — trauma and the patterns of dependency — are inseparable. If we look at the core of the term dependent-behaviour, we can see that it is essentially about always handling the difficult emotions that trauma has created.

This knowledge has been known and used for many years in systems and organisations that concern them-selves with treating individuals or families affected by addiction to alcohol, drugs, or another type of noticeable dependent behaviour. Here, an important part of the treatment is to open up and approach the feelings and to teach yourself to communicate openly about them, thus keeping the door to the feelings open. This is, amongst other things, done by regularly attending AA meetings, which many previous addicts do for the rest of their lives — years after the active addiction has ended. This comes from acknowledging that repression and denial of difficult emotions are the sources of the addiction, and if you let the repression fester, the addiction will start again. By regularly attending a forum where it is about sharing from the heart what you think and feel, you keep the door to the feelings open and the addiction in check.

Important experiences and insights of human behaviour lie in these treatment systems. Insights that we can certainly use to understand ourselves and the dynamics within our relationships — even if there is no visible alcohol or drug abuse by ourselves or the people closest to us. In our modern society, there are various things we can develop overconsumption of, and thus become addicted to, to avoid feeling the feelings within. And if we give ourselves permission to do so, we will never achieve true healing. Because the patterns of dependency will block our contact with the deep Love within, and they will block our ability to stand strong in our own life, independent and free to expand into our full potential.

So, let's have a look at how these patterns can play out in our relationships, so we are aware of them and can take care of them when they show up in our lives.

Co-dependency

Patterns of dependency often play out in a dynamic between one person whose addiction is the most visible, and then one or several close people who support the dependent behaviour — who we call the co-dependent. The way the co-dependent supports the pattern is primarily through denial of the state of things and through a lacking ability to set healthy boundaries against unhealthy behaviour. Relationships and families where one or more shop, work, workout, eat sweets or food, gamble, watch TV, drink, smoke pot, or take drugs to an excessive point can be considered under the dependent/co-dependent dynamic. But so can the less visible types where there is a distinct shut-off when it comes to talking about one's own emotions and problems. This is often paired with a distinct "know-it-all" attitude towards other people's feelings and issues. When one or several adults in a family has one of these patterns, it will always affect the healthiness of the Love and empathy with the others in one way or another. So, families where these patterns play out have to create twists of love that will inevitably disturb the wellbeing of both adults and kids. At the same time, this will also prevent the honouring of each family member's unique energy signature and thus the liberation of their true light and power.

In this way, co-dependency is used as a term for the dynamic that occurs within any dysfunctional relationship. It can be everything between emotional immaturity and lack of accountability, to active drug and alcohol addiction — and everything in between. When we look at the pattern on this broader definition, it becomes evident that it's a widespread phenomenon that stretches beyond relationships and families with visible problems with addiction. It is a phenomenon and a dynamic that occurs in a vast number of families, if not all. This is again because we, in 3D, have had so much twisted love and poor prerequisites when it comes to meeting our difficult emotions with Love and empathy, thus taking responsibility for these factors in our interaction with others. And because these compromises and twists the mutual dependency has created in our relationships is so deeply ingrained in us, it has become difficult for us to sense who we truly are and what we actually desire.

So, in 3D many of us have been in close relations where the lines between individuals have become blurry and fluid. Not from the loving unity-consciousness' point of view of how we are all connected, but from an unhealthy and fear-based awareness that wants to avoid feeling the pain within, because we don't have the tools to handle it. The parties in the relationship fill each other's holes, so to speak, in that both individual's behaviour builds on trauma from their childhood, and the sub-conscious intention with both is to avoid feeling them. With these opposite strategies in a relationship — one over-responsible and the other under-responsible — the individuals will fit together like a hand in a glove. This way, a relationship built on the co-dependent dynamic becomes a relationship where each party mirrors the other's wounds, something very widespread in 3D.

If you think back to the incident from my childhood where my mother lost it, I, in that situation, became programmed to participate in the dynamic mentioned above in my intimate relationships. Through the projection of my mother's pain on me, the fluid boundaries, irresponsibility from the adult side, and the concealment and repression following the incident, ingrained in me an overly responsible personality trait. Something was my fault — something "out there" that I certainly didn't understand but that my entire system knew I had to take responsibility for. For a large part of my adult life, this trait has meant I've been more "aware of others" than of myself, and I have wilfully taken on the responsibility for everyone's happiness to an extent that has corrupted my own wellbeing. It can sound like a Florence Nightingale martyrium, but I don't consider this a positive, let alone loving, trait. It rests on just as big an emotional closed-off-ness as the other side of the coin; the projective and under-responsible personality.

I have spent a lot of years understanding the dynamic and finding my way out of the unhealthy, twisted love, and making myself able to enter an intimate relationship where we, instead of mirroring each other's wounds, mirror each other's strengths. Precisely as 5D vibrations invite us all to do.

The Feminine and the Masculine

In my experience, there are some gender-specific characteristics within co-dependency patterns. Just like it is known within the world of abuse that most abusers are men and most enablers are women, in the softer family versions of the co-dependent dynamic there is a tendency that most people with under-responsible and projective behaviours are men, and most who behave over-responsibly and introjectively are women. And that is no surprise. First of all, as we previously mentioned, we have lived in a patriarchal society for six thousand years. And in a patriarchal society, it is by definition the men who dominate, and take up space, and who can allow themselves to agitate with projection and outwards-directed behaviour towards parties with lower status — that party being women. And the women are then told to follow, receive, and take on guilt and responsibility, which is introjective behaviourism. Secondly, it is not a surprise because this pattern is supported by the qualities that characterise the masculine and feminine energy, respectively. The masculine energy is directed outwards, while the feminine energy is directed inwards.

So, the characteristics mentioned above of the feminine and masculine energy, respectively, have been amplified by the patriarchal structure of society. It might actually be more accurate to say that it is the *lower aspects* of the masculine and feminine energy that have been amplified. Because it's those that have played out for generations in 3D, where both energies and their core interactions have been distorted. There are many reasons for this, e.g., the vibrations on Earth have been so low, the fight for survival has been so rough, and the veil between life on Earth and the true aspects of our existence have been so thick and impenetrable.

But the primary reason that it's the low and twisted aspects of both the feminine and masculine qualities that have played out in 3D is because of the consequential cut-off and suppression of the true feminine energy that life in the long-term patriarchy has resulted in. Because of this, the strong outwards directed behaviour that the masculine energy has practised has lacked both bottom and depth — qualities that should come from the masculine connecting with

*the masculine
energy is
directed
outwards,
while the
feminine
energy is
directed
inwards*

the feminine. When that connection is lost, the masculine proactivity is in imminent danger of becoming hollow, shallow, and incomplete — and of creating a life for all where the most profound aspects of life are non-existent because they aren't respected or acknowledged. The primary representations of the lower aspects of masculinity have been aggression, assault, insensitivity, dominance, oppression, and harassment of everything standing in the way of the masculine need to make things happen and having everything under control.

The introspective, empathetic, wholesomely-oriented, and cyclical qualities that are part of the feminine energy's core essence have similarly been twisted in a warped way to be heard in a system that in the end does not respect women's values. Assimilation, submission, lack of self-respect, oversensitivity, passiveness, and various neurotic patterns have been the primary representations of the lower aspects of femininity. This has meant that most of the women who have made a name for themselves in our society and that we recognise as strong women have, down the line, developed a well-functioning masculine energy. While most of us still have yet to experience what a well-functioning feminine energy actually looks and acts like. This has further meant that Love which has traditionally been a woman's domain has had tight conditions and, to a certain degree, been put under the warping of both the feminine and masculine energy, and the interaction between them, which the many love-twists is an example of.

Eradicating the Old, Establishing the New

Here on the threshold of 5D, we begin to get more and more in touch with the higher aspects of both femininity and masculinity. But first, we have to go through a deep cleanse — something we are witnessing in the MeToo movement that started in 2017 and that, at this time of writing, is entering its second wave. It exposes a plethora of masculine assaults, harassment, and abuse of power over the feminine.

This cleansing is a necessary part of the transition to 5D because it brings behavioural patterns that have occurred in the shadows into the light, so we can see them and take a stand on whether we want to continue like this. Precisely like the many exposés of and resistance against the patriarchal system's abuse of power and violence against people who don't "fit into the white man's society" that we have seen in recent years. Even if it can feel violent and can be both agonising and shocking to experience, there is no doubt in my mind that the vehement cleansing is both good and necessary. We can't build a new world with true equality between all people, hereunder the genders, and with a loving and respectful collaboration between humankind and Mother Earth, without tidying up the residue first. Just like you can't properly clean a house so it becomes new and shiny without turning on the light and digging through all the filth so it can be removed. The new energy shines with its clear and pure light on all corners so we can see and take a stand on it and, with a fully lit awareness, create a new foundation for the new world.

And the new world that is standing by the door is a world built on the equal interaction between masculinity and femininity. Despite what some fear these years, we aren't headed towards a matriarchy where the feminine dominates the masculine. Both the patriarchy and matriarchy are what anthropologist Riane Eisler in her book *The Chalice and the Blade* call domination systems, where one part of the human race rises to a rank higher than another. Even though it can look that way at the moment, and most likely will continue to do so for a few years with the considerable focus on women's perspectives we are experiencing, it is not what humankind is headed towards in the long run.

The feminine energy in these years is simply in the middle of collecting what has been lost after millennia of oppression, which can look like the beginning of a matriarchy at first. This is happening on Earth in a tangible and visible way that we can see with our very eyes. And it is happening in the more invisible levels where a lot of galactic portals in recent years have opened up for feminine energies that for millennia have been inaccessible on Earth, and now flow through to all of us. This includes the Divine Mother's energy. So we can embark on a new world where it is the end of one-sided masculine divinity, and where the divine feminine and the divine masculine co-create in complete equality. In my eyes, there is no doubt that the current visible and invisible events are connected — and that the visible to a large extent is sustained by and takes place as a result of the invisible energy-infusions. The entire universe is working towards helping Earth leave the heavy 3D vibrations and entering 5D, where the co-creation between the masculine and the feminine finds a balance, and the understanding and respect of the feminine is finally set in place and anchored.

Because in the long run, we are headed towards what Riane Eisler calls *the partnership model.* Through her research, she has discovered that this model has been much more prevalent in prehistoric societies than previously thought. It is a society where social relations are primarily based on the principle of unity instead of ranks. And where the masculine creativity and pro-activity builds on the insight of the feminine wisdom. According to the many messages that, at this time, come to Earth from the spiritual world about the future of the planet, we are furthermore moving towards a society where all humans develop both of the gender's qualities on their own. This means that the traditionally re-cognised genders, as we understand them today, are softening up more and more.

There is a foundation for Love to blossom in such a society without all the many twists that a one-sided pat-riarchy or matriarchy would inherently entail. This also goes for the patterns of dependency that Love in 3D was impacted by. And finally, there is a foundation for us to begin honouring and appreciating our individual, unique energy signatures — regardless of how it is allotted on the feminine-masculine scale and other various scales. When all is unfolded, a wealth of potential for the connections and interactions we can create together will open up.

So, let's now look at what is needed for you to carry on with this process within yourself and your life. Beyond strengthening your self-Love, as we touched on in Chapter 2, it is about training yourself to honour and appreciate your unique energy signature just as much as your creator appreciates it. To understand how valuable it is and, because of that, be true to it and let it be your guiding light in the way you live your life, independent of what your surroundings think about the choices you make.

Let us get started.

Set Peaceful Boundaries from the Heart

Some of what we have learned in 3D — and that we are still in the middle of learning in this transition to 5D — is what happens to us when we enter unhealthy and draining relationships that keep us from having the courage to stand up and shine our bright light in the world. And that's an important lesson. It has been difficult for us to navigate in complex relationships where things blend in often incomprehensible patterns. It has taught us to master ourselves in the lower polarisations of the world, and it has taught us to stand up for ourselves and protect our right to be who we are, despite pressure and criticism. And no doubt, a lot more as well.

It is in no way an insignificant lesson that we'll take with us on our evolving journey into the higher dimensions, because it is all insight we will need in our creation of the new world in 5D. I am sure our souls are happy and satisfied with the exciting developmental opportunities they have had in 3D. But I am also sure that the way we have learned these things in 3D — the hard way so to speak — is coming to an end. The time has come for us — out of Love for ourselves, each other, and our creator — to set boundaries for ourselves in peaceful and powerful manners and to take the messages that come from within seriously. So that we act on them and let them set our life's direction smoothly and thus stand with our feet planted in our own light.

Here, I want to return to your inner GPS that I presented in Chapter 2. Because the delicate, innate navigational system that works through the self-empathetic process is a really good friend to have within reach when it comes to training yourself to stand in your light. It is designed to help you make decisions from within, while simultaneously communicating your choices to others authentically and peacefully — the way Marshall Rosenberg calls *non-violent communication*. Rosenberg himself describes non-violent communication as *a language from the heart*, which I find very profound. Because when we communicate from a place of our deepest needs, what happens is that we share our heart's desire with each other. We say what is important to us, what really means something to us, what we are passionate about, and what we wish most of all. That is all our heart's desire. With that interpretation, we can expand *to speak from our needs* as we touched upon in Chapter 2, into a bigger concept which we can call *to speak from our needs, desires, values, and dreams.* Together, it makes up the big shared reservoir that is our inner drive and which I like to call the reservoir of *all that is important to me.*

So, with our unique energy signature in mind, the principle of speaking and acting from our needs/desires/values/dreams can help us appear clearly and authentically as who we really are. And it can help us say *yes* and *no* to the right things at the right time in a way that comes from our heart, and not from blaming or attacking others. When we communicate this way with ourselves — in our inner dialogue about what way we should go and what choices we should make — and with other people, we are setting boundaries from the heart. This is the opposite of how we are used to setting boundaries in 3D, which has primarily been from the mind. We are trained and taught to be conscious of our stands, opinions, rationales, and reasonings on every-thing we do. To be ready to make it known what we think of this and that — and why — has been awarded throughout our entire education and continues to be for most of us in the work-life. It means that the ego's evaluation and judgement of what is OK/not OK, right/wrong, good/bad, etc. — where we discuss something outside ourselves — has had a high status in 3D. Whereas, to speak from our self-empathetic perception of what is going on inside, and what we want, and would like, and dream of has not been so highly considered.

But when you want to start practicing being true to yourself and appreciating your unique energy signature, just as much as your creator appreciates it, it is necessary that you practise speaking from the heart. Because it's in the heart your soul and your unique energy signature resides. And the messages about what is right, true, good, important, and nourishing for you comes from the heart. They come through your inner GPS — your feelings that tell you something important about your needs/desires/values/dreams. These messages are important guidelines for the choices you make and how you communicate your choices to others, and thus how you show others who you actually are. This makes a big difference in your interaction with others. Because when we communicate with others from the heart instead of the mind, our actions become more peaceful. We do not end up in discussions about who and what is right, and who and what is not. Instead, we open up for a dialogue about who we each truly are. And when we speak from the heart, we listen to each other from the heart, not the brain. To make this process function optimally, it is necessary that we free ourselves of the mentioned patterns of dependency. Because if we are trapped in co-dependency patterns with another person, we can, of course, not have the same open and free interest in both our own and the other's needs/desires/values/dreams, and who we and they really are.

But when we lift ourselves and each other from these dependency patterns, speaking and setting boundaries from the heart we practice a form of communication that can create much more fruitful, loving, and supportive relationships with other people than our traditional communication from the mind has been able to. We come from a severely softer place, which creates a severely softer response in and from others. I have no doubt that this will be one of the big changes in how our communication — including our communication with ourselves — will play out in the future. And I also have no doubt that Marshall Rosenberg, maybe without knowing it, opened up the door for the paradigm shift when he developed this form of communication many years ago.

Saying "No" to Others and "Yes" to Yourself

When you practice speaking from the heart, it is an inevitable and necessary part that you sometimes have to say *"no"* to something that others desire and ask you for. And the more you can avoid ending up in the mind when you say *"no"*, the higher the probability others will accept and respect your *"no"* without resistance and without feeling as if it is them personally that you are rejecting and saying no to. Let us take a look at how you do this by using your inner GPS.

Let's say that someone invites you to do something on Tuesday. You might immediately sense, without fully knowing why, that you don't want to do what they suggest. You feel this through one or another form of emotional reaction from the category called *un-comfortable feelings*. It can be irritation, fear (of being caught up in something you don't want to do), anger — or just an underlying unease or resistance of sorts. This is your inner GPS-lady that's speaking to you: *Be vigilant; this might not be the right direction for you.* Here comes the first test: Are you listening to the GPS-lady's message, or do you ignore it and go along with what the other person suggested, to be friendly and avoid conflict? I hope it's the first one. Here you get to choose from two paths:

If you can immediately sense what's behind the GPS-lady's emotional unease — which need/desire/value/dream the other's invitation is colliding with — you can answer right away, i.e.:

"I would like to pass on that as I've put Tuesday aside as a writing day in my calendar."

But if you are unsure about what the GPS-lady's message is about, but can just feel that there is *something* that's bothering you, you can ask for time to be clearer about it:

"I'll need to think about it; I've got something else on Tuesday I need to check up on first."

Here, you can step aside and use the time needed for your self-empathetic process: What kind of feeling is it that's at hand — and what need/desire/value/dream is it the feeling is trying to make you aware of? When you understand that the reason behind the GPS-lady's message is your need/desire to be true to your commitment to yourself about setting aside the Tuesday to write, another test comes forth: Do you decide to stick to your commitment with yourself, or do you say yes to the invite anyway? If it's the first, you can reply just like before:

"I would like to pass on that as I've put Tuesday down as a writing day in my calendar." Or you might make yourself

even clearer by adding, *"And it is really important for me to get on with my book."*

If you hear yourself saying *"yes"* even though it doesn't fit your needs, it is a really good idea to ask yourself: *"Why am I not sticking to my commitment to myself?"*

If you, i.e., are in the middle of writing a book, ask yourself:

"Is the dream/desire about the book not important enough for me to commit to? Is it to avoid making someone else sad that I say "yes" despite my agreement with myself? Is it to avoid being perceived as self-obsessed or egotistical that I say "yes"? Is it because I am scared that the other person thinks it is ridiculous that I am writing a book? Is it because I think the other person's need is more important than my own?" All of these questions can get you reflecting upon the motive behind why you act the way you do and might help you to act in a different, more self-loving manner in the future if you realise that you didn't honour and respect your own needs/desires/values/dreams to the extent you wished to have done. Your inner GPS has helped you to be wiser about your tendency to *maybe* twist the Love for yourself. And if you choose to stick with your agreement with yourself and say *"no"* to the suggestion in the way I suggest, you solely base your *"no"* around your own need/desire/value/dream, so the other person has no reason to feel personally rejected.

If you are sitting there and thinking, *"Well, that is how I do it,"* then everything is fine — you are well on track with using your inner GPS, and you respect and act on the messages it brings you. If you are thinking, *"Yeah, I do know what my need/desire/value/dream is, but I just find it so difficult to stick to them when I'm together with other people"* then you are just like most of us. This is the most widespread test at this time. Especially for women who, by definition, have less space to move in this post-patriarchal society. We, time after time, collide with doubt about whether we are too self-centred and if we can allow ourselves to say no and set boundaries based on our own needs/desires/values/dreams. We have been taught for so long that it's *others first* — then me, that we often have to get a good and solid grip on ourselves to have the courage to insist that our needs/desires/values/dreams are just as important — in our own life, actually more important — than others. It demands training and willpower to learn that.

But 5D is calling, so there is no other way. The world needs all of us and our unique energy signatures in their untouched, pure form.

Throughout the process, it is really good and useful to remind yourself that it is the old ghosts that are at play. It is 3D's ego-ghosts that think it can be dangerous to stand out as prominently and authentically as your inner GPS is guiding you to do. They think that you are betraying others if you stand by yourself. And they think that you will be perceived as egotistical and selfish if you say no to somebody or something to honour your own needs/desires/values/dreams. It's all an illusion that belongs to the past. Your creator wants something else for you now: That you step out and shine un-apologetically, without all of the ego's veils. And the creator has provided you with your inner GPS to guide you on the way. In all of its simplicity, it is a strong tool that puts you in direct touch with your soul's voice.

I have experienced this myself throughout my own process. Some of what I benefitted the most from on my journey to reclaiming my own energy is my persistent exercising of following my inner GPS. And to practise standing by and acting on the messages it brings me. It has helped me detangle my twisted love, my co-dependency, and my need to be overly responsible for others and move home to myself. It has helped me set healthy and clear boundaries around myself and given me the courage to step more and more into my own light. All in all, it has made a massive difference for me that is difficult to fully describe. I hope you will be inspired to give your own GPS a chance to do the same in your life.

Other Ways to Honour Your Energy Signature

Besides exercising your self-empathy and inner GPS and setting boundaries from the heart, there are, of course, many other ways to be true to yourself and to honour, value, and cherish your unique energy signature.

Here, your Love for yourself is a very prominent factor. Because Love is, in reality, the biggest protector of your unique energy signature that exists. When you are filled with it, your healthy boundaries and your ability to honour and cherish your needs/desires/values/ dreams, will often come through completely on their own. You will attract energies in the form of people and events that match the Love vibration within you, which we will touch more on in Chapter 5. And these are, of course, very high vibrational energies that neither over- whelm nor drain you. So, to increase your Love for yourself is an invaluable way to be true to yourself and your unique energy signature, so you can glow and shine just as your creator wants you to. The exercises at the end of Chapter 2 will help you implement this. To decide to leave the direction of your life in the hands of your inner GPS is actually an expression of a huge Love for yourself — in the same way that to encourage loving yourself automatically means you will begin to listen to your inner GPS more and more. In that sense, it all connects in a very nice way.

As a supplement to self-Love's and self-empathy's inside-out ways of honouring and protecting your energy, there are also many outside-in ways. There are, i.e., the methods where you imagine a pillar, an egg, or a bubble of light around you, and then you set the intention that only what has your best in mind can get through the light. Or the imaginary Michelin suit which protects you from the external energies that you don't want getting through to your energy field. I won't go more in-depth about these methods since there are many sources where you can find them if you feel the need to protect your energy field against unwanted energies. Instead, we will now look at exercises and tips that you can use to take good care of yourself and your unique energy signature in the inside-out way.

EXERCISES & TIPS

The first exercise in this section is a practice in using your inner GPS to say *"no"* and to set boundaries. The first part is a bit reminiscent of the exercise in self-empathy that you received in Chapter 2, but this one takes it one step further and gives you instructions on how you can say *"no"* to and set boundaries around another person through communication. It also comes with specific suggestions on the actions Exercise 3 in Chapter 2 ends with.

Beyond that, you will receive a radical method to make sure that you don't overstep your boundaries and to never allow yourself to ignore the loving and guiding messages from your inner GPS.

And finally, you will receive the one-million-dollar question that helps you let Love lead your choices and decisions.

EXERCISE 4

Say No and Set Boundaries

Think of a situation where you need to say *"no"* or speak up to someone or about something. It can be a situation where you experience an unease in the shape of an uncomfortable feeling that tells you that you might need to honour and cherish your own needs.

Take a few deep breaths, preferably with an open mouth, so the energy settles nicely in your body, and then begin to tune into the situation.

Try to identify the feeling that's at play. Is it anger, grief, frustration, impatience — or another type of uncomfortable feeling telling you that you have a need/desire/value/dream that is not being met?

When you are in touch with the feeling, begin to feel for what's behind it — what unmet need/desire/value/dream is it that it wants to make you aware of? Here you can use the steps from Exercise 3 on self-empathy from Chapter 2.

When you have identified what the feeling wants to tell you about your needs, begin investigating how you can express yourself to another person regarding the situation. In your communication, you primarily speak about your own need/desire/

value/dream — not about the other, and not about your thoughts and judgements.

Here are a few examples of some phrases you can let yourself be inspired by:

"It is important for me that the animals I eat have had a good and free life (value), so I am saying no thanks to the beef when it isn't organic."

"I will not be spoken to in that way. I want to be treated with respect (desire)."

"I really want to have a deeper connection and talk more with you (desire), so I would like for us to turn off the television while we are eating."

"I am dreaming of a holiday in nature where there is complete peace and quiet (dream), so I'd like to look at Norway instead of the French riviera. What do you think about that?"

"I am quitting because I have to acknowledge that my need for developing (need) can't be satisfied in this organisation."

"I need an evening of total relaxation (need), so I'd like to say no thanks to the invitation on Friday."

"Being open means a lot to me (value), so I won't be part of speaking about others behind their backs."

"I need to know where this group is in regards to this problematic aspect (need), so I don't want to continue until that has been cleared up. So, could we please take a moment where we each can say how we are feeling about it?"

EXERCISE 5

Every MAYBE is a NO

This exercise can be described with very few words. But that doesn't mean it is easy to practise. In short, it is about trying to live by the mantra: *Every MAYBE is a NO.*

It is a mantra I received many years ago from a wise woman, and it was a bit of a revolution for me to begin living by it. Because I had almost lived by the opposite, which is to say that *every MAYBE is a YES.*

I was the one who always let doubt benefit others. The positive and optimistic one, bordering on the gullible and naive. So, if I was in doubt about whether something was good for me or not, I said *"yes"*. If it was good for others, then ... And that has led to me overstepping my own boundaries repeatedly.

When I began to live by that mantra, I became more assertive, more realistic, more powerful, happier, and more satisfied. In other words, truer to myself and with the energy and resources to do what my soul was meant to. And with a much stronger focus on what is *really* important; for me, my soul, and thus the world. My unique energy signature emerged step by step and allowed me to be more and more ME.

I am not saying that you necessarily have to use the mantra every time a *maybe* appears in your life. But try to live by it for a period of time, say 40 days — a magical number to create consistent changes. And then see what happens; within and around you.

EXERCISE 6

The Million Dollar Question

Here you will receive the question to help you make healthy and self-loving choices in your life.

You can, i.e., use it when you are in situations where you have to make a decision and are in doubt as to what will be the best and right choice. Or maybe when you are in doubt about how much you unconsciously blend your own needs/desires/values/dreams with others'.

It sounds like this:

"If I loved myself unconditionally, what would I do?"

The question tends to open up for the true, healthy, and self-loving choice in all the situations/dilemmas we can find ourselves in.

This is how you do it:

- Get comfortable
- Close your eyes
- Take (at least) three deep inhales and exhales, preferably through the open mouth

Connect your roots from your feet with Mother Earth's core, where her golden heart resides.

Connect your roots on the top of your head with the Divine Love in Heaven. Let the energies from Earth and Heaven meet in your Heart.

Sit for a moment and feel the connection with your Heart, Earth, and Heaven.

Think about the situation/dilemma that your decision rests on. Sense the feelings at play and the thoughts you think. When you are in touch with the situation, ask the question:

"If I loved myself unconditionally, what would I do?"

Have faith in the first answer that comes through after asking the question. Even if it sounds absolutely ridiculous (it's just your ego speaking).

The answer should ideally come within ten seconds. Anything that happens in your mind after that is in the risk zone of overthinking.

If you didn't get an answer within ten seconds, then proceed with your day and trust that the answer will appear — maybe at an unexpected moment and in an unexpected way. It can be when you are sleeping, waking up, walking, cleaning, or something similar.

But have faith that the answer will come. Because it will. Your most important task is to be awake, listen closely, and have the courage to act on it when it appears.

CHAPTER 4

FORGIVENESS AND GRATITUDE

Two Vital Paths Towards Love

When you are working towards reclaiming Love as a fundamental aspect of your life, there are, beyond what we have already touched on, various ways that can help you. This chapter is about two of them: Forgiveness and Gratitude. Actually, these two ways are not only ways that *can* help you — I would go as far as to say that these are two vital paths that you *have* to allow to help you. Because without both forgiveness and gratitude, it can be very difficult to get the Love vibration anchored as your vibrational base. Let me try to briefly tell you Why.

Forgiveness is a path that is necessary to walk down because it simply lightens your entire system. When we venture out on this journey where we throw away the old 3D patterns, what happens is that your frequency rises. Because Love is one of the highest vibrational emotions that exist and it lies all the way at the top of the vibrational ladder — or at the top of the emotional guidance scale, as Abraham-Hicks' teachings call it. This is just two ways of expressing the same thing. So, an unavoidable and utmost pleasant part of bringing your system towards the direction of 5D's Love frequency is to lighten your system and move up the vibrational ladder. But if you carry low vibrating feelings — such as anger, rage, irritation, powerlessness, bitterness, guilt, shame, etc. — about something that happened in the past or is happening in the present, then climbing this ladder can be really difficult.

You will typically see that your ability to practise true Love does develop and your frequency moves upwards, but that you slide down the ladder again and lose the connection to the Love vibration. It might be replaced by some low vibrating feelings, such as the ones mentioned above, because it is impossible to be filled with Love and the mentioned feelings simultaneously — they are simply too far apart on the vibrational ladder for it to be possible. When you forgive everything that has happened in the past — including yourself — the low vibrating feelings that have resided in your subconscious system will no longer be able to keep your frequency down. They lose their power, so to speak, and you set both yourself and others free. And from that state of liberation, it is much easier for you to develop and maintain the connection to Love. More on that in a bit.

Gratitude is a path that is also necessary to walk down because it's a shortcut that automatically brings you in direct touch with Love. The two emotions vibrate on pretty much the same frequency, so when you decide to introduce a gratitude practice in your day-to-day life, you simultaneously decide to connect with Love. And you choose to connect yourself with a range of other states of emotions that find themselves close to gratitude and Love — such as trust, joy, clarity, and strength. So, to nourish gratitude grants you a sort of multipack, so to speak, that inherently brings along many other wonderful feelings, including Love. We can also say it like this: Just like it is impossible to be bitter and hateful at the same time as being filled with Love, it is also impossible to be grateful and trusting and not be filled with Love. That is what understanding frequencies and the knowledge of the vibrations of our emotions tells us. And perhaps our life experiences have told us the same many times as well?

Practising gratitude daily and sharpening your awareness of everything in life that you have reason to be grateful for, is a really good friend to have with you on your journey to reclaim Love. It brings you in direct touch with the very magic of the creator and awakens your sense of the wonderful and miraculous nature of life, as well as Love and empathy for all that is alive, yourself included. We will explore how it all connects and how you do this at the end of the chapter.

The Vibrational Ladder

Gratitude, joy, Love, trust
Clarity, freedom, intuitive wisdom, strength
Excitement, passion
Eagerness, enthusiasm, fortune
Belief, optimism, positive expectations
Hope, satisfaction
Boredom, pessimism
Frustration, impatience, irritation
Disappointment, doubt, overwhelm, worry
Anger, blame, control, discouragement, self-righteousness
Hate, jealousy, rage, revenge
Feeling caged, guilt, self-sacrifice, shame, worthlessness
Depression, despair, disparity, fear, grief, powerlessness

Inspired by Gill Edwards and Abraham-Hicks.

FORGIVENESS — A MULTIFACETED MATTER

There are several things I want you to consider when you are thinking about starting a forgiveness process in your life. Because some of the ways we have understood and interpreted life in our 3D consciousness look quite different when we upgrade and look at them from 5D. The upgrades and changes to your understanding and interpretation can be a defining insight on both whether you set a forgiveness process into action or not and your ability to actually *complete* the process, so you really set yourself and others free from the past.

The first thing I will ask you to consider is something I have mentioned many times in this book already — your soul itself, before it was incarnated for this cycle, desired to experience the challenges you have endured. There exist many different terms for this concept, e.g., soul contracts, before-birth commitments, and soul commitments. These are all about how our souls have entered into agreements about which interactions we wish to have with others in the earthly incarnation, and which roles we each will play in each other's lives. All to reach the optimal conditions to develop the specific qualities that the soul, in its eternal journey of expansion, wants.

Before we go any further, I want to tell you a story from one of my courses in self-Love. An attendant, Birthe, said to me halfway through the course, *"I have realised that the thing about learning to love myself is actually Plan A, and not Plan B, as I used to think."* I love this expression and I have used it many times since to make what this is really all about more comprehensible. What Birthe was saying is that many of us, for many years, have worked on developing our self-Love as a Plan B — essentially as an emergency plan for when Plan A hadn't worked out. And Plan A was, in that regard, that our parents should have given us unconditional Love and support since childhood, which they couldn't because of their own traumas and wounds. Because of that, we had to turn to Plan B, where we provided ourselves with the Love we missed out on. But maybe it really is the other way around. Maybe it was part of the agreement with our parents' souls that we *shouldn't* receive unconditional Love, so we instead could learn to love ourselves. And maybe our most important and significant task is precisely to learn to love and appreciate ourselves, as the creator loves and appreciates us, so we can bring our Love all the way home and merge with our essence. In that perspective this is Plan A. I think that's an interesting thought.

I know that it can be a difficult concept to take in, especially for those who might have experienced violent assaults, abuse, and betrayal, maybe even from early childhood. And one of the most important things to be aware of in grasping and digesting this concept is that you don't use it towards yourself like the ego would. Something sounding like this, *"I asked for it, so it is my own fault,"* or *"Then all of it is my responsibility,"* would be an oversimplified and insufficient way to understand the utmost complex dynamic that has taken place and is still taking place between souls in the universe and individuals in 3D's heavy vibrations.

So, you have to find a way to tackle the thought that your soul, on some deep level, wanted the challenges. Take responsibility for your part in it — and at the same time be true to your inner GPS that tells you there was something that wasn't right, and that it's something you have to make sure you don't expose yourself to anymore. And in addition to this, stand up for yourself by speaking up against others' violating actions through clear and direct words from the heart, as we touched on in Chapter 3. In order to protect your own energy — and maybe move away from the violating situations and people if they are still in your life. It can be complicated to balance and one of the paradoxes we have to learn to embrace at this time. We are in the middle of replacing the ego's dualistic black and white view on things with a more nuanced look that's more in tune with the truth of what's happening in our earthly lives. At the same time, it also brings us important insight on how we can take full responsibility for ourselves, our actions, and our life, and how to let others take responsibility for themselves, their actions, and their life. When we have mastered this complicated balance, we will be well prepared to step into 5D.

This brings us to the next thing I want you to take into consideration in regards to forgiveness, which is the question: *"What have I learned from the situation?"* This is what I like to call *searching for the gift*. Because regardless of how violent and inhumane the experiences we carry in our luggage are, there is always a gift to be found. Louise Hay is one of the best examples of this. She had a childhood that I would call unbearable, with a stepfather who abused her in the worst ways possible. Louise developed cancer at an early age and healed herself through a complete transformation of her way of being in the world. The most central parts of this process were to reprogramme her subconsciousness with positive affirmations, strengthen her self-Love, forgive the past, and develop a deep sense of gratitude for life. And everything she learned through her healing process, she used for the rest of her life. Partly to live a wonderful life, as she said, and partly to found the publishing company Hay House — the world's biggest spiritual publishing house with a wealth of books and materials that have helped millions of people all around the world to heal themselves and their lives. Amongst those countless publications is, of course, Louise's own books, where the first one is quite simply called *You Can Heal Your Life.*

So, the gift Louise Hay received from her unbearable childhood was to learn and encounter the deep potential for healing, which taking full responsibility for everything in one's life entails. Hereunder healing and transforming the wounds and trauma that her childhood had left her with, and which had made her ill. In this way, she became a glowing example which shows that healing and transformation are possible for us all. A glowing example of what Margit Madhurima Rigtrup, in her book *Det Intelligente Hjerte* (EN: *The Intelligent Heart*), expresses this way: *"Your biggest wound is your biggest gift."*

The gifts I have received from the emotional conditions of my childhood are down the road reminiscent of Louise Hay's gifts. My work untangling myself from the co-dependent and overly responsible personality traits that I have fought with for most of my adult life has brought me to some of the same conclusions as Louise Hay. Which is that there are four pillars in the process of healing:

- To rise above my ego's fearful thoughts
- To learn to love me as my creator loves me
- To realise that my soul has wanted these challenges I have gone through, and I can thus calmly forgive everything
- To realise that life and the universe supports and guides me in incredible ways — to the extent that my heart spills over with awe and gratitude

Bearing in mind that I've been inspired by Louise Hay throughout my journey for so many years, maybe it isn't so weird that I have discovered some of the same secrets around healing and transformation. However, I don't believe that is the most likely reason for us to have arrived at the same conclusions. In fact, I actually believe that it is because we, on our individual journeys, both — as with many others within the self-develop-ment world — have met some universal truths that go for all of us, regardless of what childhood trauma and soul wounds we carry. Universal truths that we all need to know as we liberate ourselves by letting go of 3D, and

*your biggest
wound
is your
biggest gift*

thus the past, and move into 5D. And as I attempt in my own way to bring to you through this book.

The third thing I will ask you to consider is a misconception of forgiveness that I have learned is quite widespread — that *forgiveness is the same as acceptance of the actions that have hurt you*. If it is connected that way in your system, then it is obvious that there will be an immense resistance against forgiving. Because that would then mean that your forgiveness legitimises the violation, betrayal, and assault someone has exposed you to. But fortunately, it is not connected that way. You forgive not to legitimise someone else's actions or remove their responsibility for their actions. You forgive to liberate yourself because the person it hurts the most, if you do not forgive, is you. It can, of course, also affect another person if it is a living person near you who senses your rage and bitterness when you see each other. But you are the one who 24/7 has to live with the unease of the low vibrating emotions that the lack of forgiveness creates. And you are the one who has to live with these emotions preventing you from climbing the vibrational ladder, thus preventing you from touching Love, joy, trust, gratitude, and excitement.

So, there are plenty of reasons for you to practise finding a way to speak up against those violating acts, protect yourself from being close to them, and at the same time work on forgiving them. When you decide to seek your own way of handling this balance, you might benefit from my experience: The more I set boundaries and honour myself and my energy, the easier it is for me to forgive. Because when I have found myself in a muddy landscape, filled with doubt and insecurity about who is responsible for what, and what I can allow myself to speak up about and what I can't, it is pretty much impossible and actually — might I say — inappropriate to forgive. Because then it appears as if I am simply opening up for even more pain through forgiveness. On the other hand, when I set clear boundaries on the foundation of self-Love, dare to stand up for myself, and am fully set on meeting the consequences of the boundaries I set down, it becomes much easier for me to forgive. It is as if self-Love, self-respect, and self-empathy have to be in place before the clarity and freedom of forgiveness can and should find their way. That is why this chapter comes after the introduction to self-Love, self-empathy, and being true to yourself.

All of the things I have asked you to consider about forgiveness are ways that often will make the forgiveness process start in itself. They bring us out of the ego's locked-up way of thinking — that we are victims to an unjust fate, that someone has done something unforgivable to us, that we bring incurable darkness and weight with us from our childhood which prevents us from creating a good life, and that we have to hold on to anger and bitterness to protect ourselves from being violated, betrayed, and assaulted again. So, give yourself time to let these considerations simmer in your system, and dig a bit into your subconscious and conscious understanding of what and who you want to forgive. And when you are ready, if you sense a need for it, you can start on a more goal-oriented path of forgiveness which you can get inspiration from in the following section and in the upcoming Exercises & Tips.

Set Yourself and Others Free

For many of us, the thought that our souls themselves wanted the challenges we have experienced brings up the notion that one of the first people we need to forgive is ourselves. Because if we have asked for it, then it's really us who are responsible for all the pain we have experienced, and the pain we may have carried over to our children as a result of our own soul wounds and trauma. It can be a heavy burden to carry. And it can cause a shift from being angry and bitter towards others, to being angry and bitter towards ourselves — and, perhaps on top of that, a feeling of guilt. This is not a healthy cocktail, so it is all the more reason to start on the path of forgiving ourselves.

If you are experiencing this, it is important to remind yourself about the old mantra: *All is Well*. With that, I mean that despite not being able to see it from our earthly perspective, there are many good — and loving — reasons that we have partaken in this painful game with each other in 3D. In that way, there is, in the end, no one who has reason to feel either guilt, anger, or bitterness towards anyone, including ourselves. Many of us have come to heal Mother Earth's trauma and pain patterns. And many have come to heal the trauma and pain patterns of humankind. And then others have come to heal a bunch of other types of trauma and pain patterns. Regardless of what the motive and mission are with our present incarnation, it is happening for everyone by first taking on the trauma and pain patterns which, for most, occurred in childhood. Through our healing of them in our own life, we at the same time heal our ancestral lineage, humankind and the planet. Participating in this painful game is thus an important part of the healing process that is happening across the world at this time through the transition from 3D to 5D. Here you really need to hold the ego's judgement of yourself and others on a tight leash, and connect to the soul's wiser, loving, and empathetic side. Because none of us can see the meaning of what all of this is, so it's good to remind ourselves that *All is Well*.

If you carry anger and bitterness towards others that have done things to you that you suffer from and struggle to forgive, there are several things I would encourage you to be aware of. The first thing is that you don't ask too much of yourself. The ego's impatience and critical sense would do something like that. The ego can certainly start to hit you in the head with thoughts, e.g., how you should already have forgiven them ages ago, or how you need to get yourself together and move on. The soul, however, knows that forgiveness of the painful experiences can, and should, take time, and that it's important to give yourself space and patience to work through the things that need to be processed before you are ready to forgive.

The next thing I will encourage you to be aware of is to make sure that you don't beat yourself up with your knowledge of the connection between feelings and vibrations. Because it can easily make you scared or scold yourself for your low vibrating feelings, when you have the knowledge that it is impossible to meet the vibration of Love and make it your fundamental vibration when you carry heavy feelings. Again, it is only the ego who would have such an insensitive approach to something so difficult. Because your heavy feelings have, like all other emotions, their full eligibility in your inner GPS — which is to tell you that there is a need/desire/value/dream that was/is not met in certain situations or relationships. So, if you experience this rollercoaster ride down the vibrational ladder that I mentioned earlier, it is all the more reason to first acknowledge and honour your feelings, be interested in their message, and from thereon do what you can to act in a way that meets the need/desire/value/dream that's behind them. That's the best way to heal the heavy feelings in a durable way.

If the heavy feelings come from past incidents — perhaps a betrayal or a violation by your parents in your childhood — you can do everything possible to be your own loving and compassionate parent, as we touched on earlier. This will help your inner child realise that there *is* now someone who listens, and sees their pain, and is interested in healing and protecting the child within you. If the feelings originate from an interaction with a person you have an active relationship with, it can be necessary to confront this person on how you experience their behaviour. And it can be necessary to remove yourself from the person if you have a close relationship with them and the behaviour continues.

Thus, there are many ways you can take action that signals to your inner child that you now take their pain seriously, and that you won't allow further violation and insensitivity towards both the child and your adult self. Only when you have spent the time you need on that process will you be ready to seriously forgive.

It should also be said that, in your process of forgiveness, it can be very valuable to remind yourself that there is no one — as in *no one* — that thrives on you continuing to carry heavy feelings from the past which are not forgiven. In fact, everyone — as in *everyone* — will prosper from you forgiving and then lifting your own frequency. Because even if it can feel as if we are protecting ourselves and are doing something good for ourselves by holding onto the pain of the past, the exact opposite is happening. If you do not set yourself free from the past and instead continue to live at the bottom of the vibrational ladder, you will continue to grow your life from that vibrational level and you will attract more of what matches your heavy feelings. Becaue *same attracts same*, which we will go into more depth on in the next chapter.

So, forgiveness means a lot to your possibility of creating a future which is not defined by your past. A future where the vibrations of your true essence and unique energy signature — and not your parents' or grandparents' vibrations — decide what you attract. Beyond that, you also bring huge gifts to your closest — both those that have betrayed and violated you, and others you are close to — when you lift your vibrations through forgiveness. Because your higher vibrations will automatically affect everyone around you. Finally, your forgiveness brings the gift of freedom to humanity, Mother Earth, and all of the universe, because we are all connected in one big vibrational field. And when one individual lifts their vibrations, it affects the whole field for the better. Like a butterfly that flutters its wings on one side of the globe, which releases a storm on the other side. You and your vibration are just as powerful in the big picture.

From Forgiveness to Gratitude

Beyond the many gifts forgiveness can bring along, my experience is that forgiveness often spills over to gratitude. In many ways, the two are inseparable. Because when I shift my experience of being a victim of my mother's inability to treat me with unconditional Love, to an experience of participating in a wonderful evolutionary dance where everything is about me reclaiming the Love for myself — Plan A, as you know — I am filled with gratitude for my mother. On a soul level, she has said yes to playing that role. Firstly, to arrive to a family in the 1920s and be the sixth of six children with everything that brings in terms of lack of attention, Love, and empathy towards her. And after

*the highest
form of
forgiveness is
to realise that
there is
nothing to
forgive*

that, playing the role of a mother without genuine abilities to love and empathise. A role that doesn't leave the most glowing legacy one could wish for. All to participate in the healing process that has been going on on Earth for many years, which culminates with the paradigm shift we are experiencing right now when we slowly begin to realise what has actually been happening. When I see my own history in that light, I feel grateful for my mother. Grateful for the opportunities she gave me to reclaim Love and the ability to learn to love myself as my creator loves me, thus playing my role in the big healing process of Mother Earth and humanity. And then I think back to Mira Kelley's regression with Serena which teaches us about the important role each of us play with our unique energy-signature.

And then I reach the same realisation as the scriptures of *A Course In Miracles* and many other forgiveness teachers, who express: *The highest form of forgiveness is to realise that there is nothing to forgive.* My mother, my father, myself nor anyone else has done anything that calls for forgiveness in the big picture. We have all played our role in life's big game to bring humanity back to itself. Back to Love. *All is well.* It does not call for forgiveness, but for wonder and gratitude. On that note, I want to suggest that we start to replace the word *forgiveness* with *liberation*. Both in our inner dialogue and in our conversations with each other. Because forgiveness is rooted so deeply in the ego's belief that some are evil and others are good. That some individuals on Earth are qualified to judge who have done wrong and who have done right. That some need forgiveness and others have the right to give it. I don't believe that's how it works. I believe it's much more complex and that it will soon be shown that the ego's dualistic interpretation of the world is much more limited and incorrect than we ever could have imagined.

This doesn't mean that, in our move from 3D to 5D, we shouldn't do everything we can to acknowledge and liberate the pain of the past within ourselves. But beginning to understand the path of forgiveness as a process where we set both ourselves and everyone else free from the low vibrating game we have had going on with each other, is a much more open and less judgemental approach to it all than the traditional perception of forgiveness. A more soul-based and less ego-based approach — and in that sense, something that's much closer to the spirit of the 5D energy. There are a couple of exercises on this at the end of this chapter.

Gratitude — Your Shortcut to Love

As I mentioned at the beginning of this chapter, practicing gratitude is a direct shortcut to Love. To understand how the shortcut works and why, let's look at what focusing on the good actually does to you.

When you turn your attention towards the good in life, you will begin to decide what your consciousness focuses on and avoids focusing on. Because life is filled with lots of different things and our consciousness exists in a constant selection process. Especially in these years, where the accessible information dump from the Internet has exploded. There is a need for us to pick and choose all the time. Your decision to focus on the good that you meet steers your attention in the direction of a more positive focus. More general attention to good news, people, and experiences is a really good step towards lifting your vibrations and bringing you upwards on the vibrational ladder. That's what we can call a positive or optimistic view on life that will make you look for the gift in all you experience and have experienced, as I touched on regarding forgiveness. An optimistic view on life often rests on the mantra *All is Well* and tends to flip any situation and experience towards the positive, instead of the negative. The difference between an optimistic and pessimistic view on life can be expressed in a statement I learned many years ago: *An optimist sees the opportunity in every challenge, a pessimist sees the challenge in every opportunity.*

So, you will have some great support on your journey of reclaiming Love if you are provided with such a view on life, either because you were born with it or because you have worked consistently to ingrain it in your consciousness. It brings you upwards on the vibrational ladder in a completely natural way in many situations, whereas others with a negative or pessimistic view on life would slide down. When you consciously decide to incorporate a gratitude practice in your life, you take this mechanism one step further. You quite simply give your mind a new task that involves consistently looking for things, experiences, and phenomena that gives you a reason to be grateful. For many of us, it is necessary to exaggerate this search for a long period of time to neutralise the inner mistake checker that is often very well-developed in our mind. Eckhart Tolle expressed this very well when he said: *"If you found yourself in paradise, it wouldn't be long before your mind would say "yes, but ..."'*

Because of that, it can be a good idea to start exaggerating and practising an extreme gratitude to see what change it can bring you. An extreme gratitude practice can be, as Pam Grout suggests in her book *Thank and Grow Rich*, when you get out of bed, stand steady on both your legs, stretch out your arms and declare loud and clear: *"Today, something absolutely life-changing is going to happen to me."* Since I am a big believer in gratitude-prayers I would add: *"Thank you for this absolutely life-changing experience that is on its way into my life today."* The term *absolutely life-changing* may not be a natural part of your vocabulary. Still, it is exactly using such an exaggerated and inflated expression that helps wake up your mind to life's magic and miracles. It takes you out of the greyscale consciousness that we often walk around with in our day-to-day life when we forget that we, in reality, live in one big miracle. If you, at the same time, supplement your declaration with an expressive body movement, like extending your arms, stamping the floor, or some type of dance move, then you are sending a strong signal to both your subconscious mind and the universe that there is will and power behind your declaration. And you are prepared for magic, and miracles, and the absolute life-changing things they are ready to bring you. At the end of this chapter, you will have an exercise to kickstart this practice to allow the *absolutely life-changing* to come into your life even more.

I mentioned that I am a big believer in praying by giving thanks, and that's another thing I will strongly encourage you to incorporate into your gratitude practice. Gratitude prayers are very powerful because they derive from a high vibration. While *please help me* prayers come from an insecure and powerless place within you, gratitude prayers come from a part of you that trusts and is sure that help has already been given and will show itself soon enough. The two types of prayers are sent from different places on the vibrational ladder, and since we receive what we radiate, prayers will either enforce your vibration from the top or bottom of the ladder. So when you ask for help, you might want to consider if it makes sense to replace *"Dear God, help me ..."* with *"Dear God, thank you for helping me ..."* Or *"I can't figure/make it through this ..."* with *"Thank you for helping me figure/make it through this ..."* I am convinced that you can feel the difference in your own system when you start to work with gratitude prayers in this way. And you can naturally pray to whoever makes the most sense for you to pray to. God, Allah, your guardian angel, other angels, your higher self,

Mohammad, Virgin Mary, Jesus, Buddha, your grandmother, or anyone else you feel connected to.

A really good activity to incorporate when you decide to start a gratitude practice is to write. The physical act of writing — and preferably so with a pen or pencil on a piece of paper — helps to anchor your awareness of what you are grateful for. So, even if it is important and recommended that you focus on gratitude many times throughout the day in your thoughts, it is a good idea to accompany this with five to ten minutes of writing every day. There are many ways you can do this. The most well-known and used is the *gratitude diary*, where you write three, five, or ten things that you are grateful for on that day every night before bedtime — the amount is up to you. Beyond that, you can write other things of gratitude, like your prayers of thanks that we touched on earlier. The gratitude diary works really well because it forces your attention to focus, in an attainable way, on finding three/five/ten good and positive things every day. Even if it feels difficult and challenging initially, trust me — it will become easier and more fun as time goes on. Because this practice forces the attention to continue finding good and wondrous things. Even when you think that there is nothing more to find, several things will still appear because you are focusing on it until you reach your three/five/ten things. And it speaks for itself that the more positive things you decide to find and write about every day, the more the mechanism starts to work.

What happens when you practise this is that you bring yourself closer and closer to the magical, miraculous, wondrous, and glorious — which we can call the *absolute life-changing* — work of the creator. Because you have to move down to the small and often overlooked details of life when you decide to keep going and find phenomena and experiences you are grateful for. So, when you *have* written about the big things you are happy for and insist on continuing, your focus begins to fall on the more mundane things you previously didn't realise you were grateful for. And for each thing you find, the more you open your heart's joy for all that lives. All the details of the creator's work becomes subject to your attention, admiration, and gratitude.

And the process naturally opens up for Love. You will fall in love with everything when you, through your grateful attention, open your eyes to the myriad of wonder that life entails. Because when it comes to it, that is what life is. A wonder. A miracle. Filled with magic. You probably know the feeling of seeing a little child, a puppy, or a mother duck and her ducklings which opens and melts your heart right there and then. When you develop attention for life's wonders, you will start to see all you meet in your way as heart-opening miracles that awake compassion and Love within you, and they will instinctively bring a little smile forth on your lips.

The little ant with a pine needle on its back. The plant that, after a frosty winter, grows its first light green leaf that will become a wealth of red dahlias in the late summer. The sperm and the egg that becomes a little human child with its own complete character and within three years can walk, run, talk, think, and wonder. That we, throughout life, will "randomly" meet people that teach and show us invaluable things on an amazing and unfathomable adventure with villains and heroes, angels and demons, kings and queens. That we love some people so deeply and profoundly that we would go through fire and water for them. It is all a myriad of wonders. And when you teach yourself to pay attention through your gratitude practice, you will SEE life as it is. You don't just let the wonders float by and take them for granted, as we often do day-to-day, but you decide to SEE them and value them. That is what a gratitude practice can do, which is why it is a shortcut to Love. Because when you truly see how incredible life is and how you are part of it, it becomes impossible to not love.

As an illustration of this, I have been allowed to feature a few verses of gratitude from Anja Steensig's *Book of Solace,* which I think expresses that exact astonishment and humility that a focus on the gratitude of small and big things in life brings out in us. As you read it, I feel confident that you will feel your vibration come in tune with the vibrations of Love and gratitude of life.

Gratitude Poem

Today I woke up to a marvelous sight
Unfolding in front of my eyes
As if layers of dust had been washed from my
gaze
And a new world appeared from the guise

I saw glorious cobwebs all covered in pearls
The treasure of dew in the morning
I saw blood-coloured leaves in a breathtaking
dance
Surrendering as they were falling

I saw sun rays of gold on a blue morning sky
Dressing clouds in a fairytale gown
I saw crystals of frost cover birches and oaks
Majestically worn as their crown

I saw people in colours like never before
All beaming with light from within
I saw kindness, compassion and truth in their
hearts
Recognized by my soul as my kin

May this morning forever stay clear in my mind
To remind me on days that are harder
Of the spirit around me, though kept out of sight
Still blessing my soul with its ardour

EXERCISES & TIPS

Here you will first receive two exercises to help you in your process of forgiving and liberating yourself and others of the past. The first is a meditative exercise where you will visualise a garden as the perfect scenery to set yourself and others free from negative bonds. The other is a checklist, which you can use throughout your path to forgiveness to keep track of how it is going.

Finally, you will see the previously mentioned exercise that helps you kickstart a gratitude practice in your life, by embracing various daily practises where you focus on the absolute life-changing things that are and will be in your life.

EXERCISE 7

The Garden of Liberty

You can do this exercise with people who aren't here on Earth anymore, people who are on Earth but no longer in your life, and people that are still in your life. The state of your relationship to those you invite into the garden of liberty does not matter, because the liberation happens within you and does not involve the others on a physical level.

This is how you do it:
Sit or lay down somewhere you won't be disturbed. Close your eyes. Take a few deep breaths, where you inhale lightness and exhale heaviness.

When you have calmed your system, begin to envision the most beautiful garden you can imagine. See the flowers, plants, trees, birds, animals, crystals, colours, fountains, and everything else in place. Create a garden in your mind that is perfect for you to let freedom and Love into all of your relationships. You can imagine that this is your 5D garden.

Now see yourself sitting at a bench in the middle of the garden. In your thoughts, invite the first person you wish to set yourself free from. See the person walking, light and happy, towards you. You rise, just as light and happy, and meet the person with kindness.

For a moment, you stand and look each other in the eyes. Then step forward and extend your arms to embrace them. If it is a comforting thought, imagine your hearts connecting. While you embrace each other, calmly say to yourself or out loud: *"I set you free and I set myself free"* three times. If the word *forgive* makes more sense for you, you can also say: *"I forgive you and I forgive myself."*

After this, let go of each other and kindly bid goodbye. The person turns around and leaves the garden even lighter and happier, just as you are. Feel the freedom, lightness, and joy within.

If you want, you can now invite another person into your garden of liberty and repeat the process. Or you can open your eyes and go on with your day, and invite others into your garden another time.

It might be a good idea to repeat the process several times with the same people if you feel that something still needs to be released. And it can be a really good idea to invite yourself, e.g., a version of you from the past, to the garden.

Do what is right and comfortable for you.

EXERCISE 8

Three Steps to Check if You Have Forgiven

Forgiveness in the good and liberating way happens from the heart, not the brain. We can most certainly decide — with the brain — that we now forgive another person without the actual liberation in the heart taking place.

That's why it is a good idea to check every now and then if we actually have forgiven who and what we *think* we have forgiven. To do an open and honest reality check on if what we have done has worked, or if some things are still unresolved that we can free ourselves from.

Below are three steps to complete a reality-check on your forgiveness process.

Step 1: Do you feel relieved?

The first step you can take is to thoroughly scan your body and your entire system to see if a proper sense of relief is present.

True forgiveness leaves a sense of relief in your body and energy system. A feeling of something being let go of and some burden disappearing. This "something" might have weighed down on you, perhaps even since childhood or youth, perhaps just within recent years.

Step 2: Which feelings are triggered when you think about the one you want to forgive?

In this step, we get more specific. When you think about the person you wish to forgive and the situations where violations took place, which feelings does it bring out in you? It is important to be completely honest with yourself here — for your own wellbeing — so you can get a candid look at whether you have forgiven from the heart and not just the brain.

I highlight this because we humans are incredibly good at storing away those feelings that aren't politically correct, especially within the spiritual world where there is a tendency for certain feelings to not be allowed, because you then won't look at yourself as "aware", "spiritual", or "pure" enough. This means that we often won't even let ourselves feel what is actually at play. We stay in our heads and decide that we have forgiven, that we don't feel rage, frustration, bitterness, hate — without ever really going into where the feelings reside.

It is a way of tricking ourselves. First of all, we can't harvest the gift of forgiveness in the form of bigger freedom, and second of all, because those feelings continue to rummage in our subconscious and drive us from there. Maybe even without us knowing. It is self-sabotaging.

On the other hand, when we allow ourselves permission to feel the way we do, we allow ourselves to be liberated. This means we are grounded in our bodies and we give ourselves permission to feel the anger, hate, bitterness, fear, insecurity, etc., if it is still there.

A lot of forgiveness work happens in stages. We often have to feel our way through several layers over time to let go of deep wounds and violations. It is entirely normal and natural — especially if it's close and prolonged relationships we are working with. That is why it's a good idea to do this reality check often.

So, if you feel the residue of old, burdensome feelings when you think about a person or situation, you know that there is still something that needs to be met with self-Love and self-empathy. And you know that it pays off to continue with your liberation work.

You can do this by going through *The Garden of Liberty* exercise several times, combined with repeating the mantra *"I forgive you, and I forgive myself,"* or *"I set you free and I set myself free"* every time thoughts about the person or incident emerges in your everyday life.

Step 3: What have you learned from the situation and person?

The last step is to ask yourself:

- What have I learned from the person who violated me?
- What have I learned from the situations/conflicts/interactions with this person?
- What gift can I harvest from my interactions with this person?

When you can answer these questions with an honest heart and without anger, grief, hate, irritation, or bitterness, you can be pretty sure that what you have done to forgive has actually worked. Because then you have moved from *"It is someone else who has violated/is violating me,"* to *"We have had an interaction with each other that has left me with an important lesson."*

Those are two very different places and the movement from one to the other shows that you have taken an essential step in taking responsibility for the experiences you have and have had. You realise that there has been a reason for everything, which might, in reality, be a gift.

EXERCISE 9

Kickstart Your Gratitude Practice

This exercise is inspired by Pam Grout's encouragement to exaggerate your gratitude by developing your excitement of life and by searching for *absolutely life-changing* things. This is an approach that is really effective in awakening your attention from the greyscale everyday-consciousness — where the miracles and wonders of life are taken for granted — to the awake and alive consciousness that views life as the magnificent and magical adventure it truly is.

I encourage you to buy or create your own personal book of gratitude and spend forty days where you integrate the following three elements into your everyday life:

- Each morning as you get out of bed, stand with steady feet, extend your arms (or another movement), and declare loudly three times: *"Today, something absolutely life-changing is on its way into my life."*
- In the evening before bedtime, write three (or five or ten if you're ambitious) absolutely life-changing things that have happened throughout the day in your book of gratitude. Remember to search

for the small things that you usually wouldn't perceive as magnificent but that you, with your new consciousness, begin to see as tiny miracles.
- In the evening before bedtime, write in your book of gratitude one or more prayers of gratitude that attract what you wish to bring into your life.

Here are a few examples:

Dear Angels, thank you for making me aware of the new perfect home, that is waiting for me …

Dear Divine Love, thank you for showing me my dream job …

Dear Buddha, thank you for helping me support my mum through her illness in the most compassionate way …

Keep an open eye out for which signals and impulses you receive regarding a new home, job, the relationship with your mum, etc. Because often, the help we get comes from our own insight and instincts — not necessarily as a voice, a picture, or an offer from other people. The key is to recognise and trust the help, regardless of how it shows itself.

When you have completed this practice for forty days, and ideally for the rest of your life, I do dare to promise that you'll open your mind to new nuances and details around what you have reason to be grateful for. And you will have an overflowing bible in your book of gratitude that you can always pull up and let yourself be invigorated by on the dark and heavy days where you need to be reminded of the Love and magic in life.

You can, of course, always write other things in your book of gratitude than what I have suggested when you feel inspired to do so.

CHAPTER 5

CREATE AS LOVE

Your Life is as You Are

It is not a coincidence that the title of this chapter is *Create As Love* and not *Create With Love,* as we might have said in 3D. Because, as the subtitle suggests, some of what we are beginning to understand in 5D about creation is that the process happens from the inside-out. The life we create for ourselves reflects who we are and what our inner state is like — more than it reflects how good we are at using various principles and methods of manifestation. We can also phrase it like this: Everything we attract reflects the vibration we, ourselves, are filled with — and the vibration is closely connected with our emotional state of being. Let's take a closer look at how it all connects.

The first, and most important, thing to know regarding creation is that *you are a creator*. That is the basis of you and all other human beings' existence. When our souls were created, the creator left a part of their essence with us, and thus we, each and all, carry the creator's essence. Just like we, here in our earth-bound lives, carry our parents' and whole lineage's essence through genes and DNA. It means that we can't help but create, and that we 24/7 — whether we know it or not — are taking part in creation processes that all together shape our lives. But how do these creation processes work? In this regard it makes sense to me to view myself as a send-and-receive-station. I stand and *you are*

a creator

walk here on Earth, and send out a signal picked up by the universe which sends something back that matches what I, myself, sent. In that way, a constant exchange between me and the universe is taking place. This exchange happens through the Law of Attraction, which I assume you have heard of. It is one of the most important cosmic laws to know when we want to understand how we are shaping our lives.

When you think of yourself as this send-and-receive station, it becomes clear that it is impossible to *not* create. Because the exchange that is taking place between you and the universe is just as impossible to step out of as the Law of Gravity: When you hold an object with heavier mass than air and let go, it falls to the ground. It is the same with the Law of Attraction: You can only receive something that resonates with the frequency you project. That is how this universal law is set; it is an unavoidable premise. Here I feel urged to add that there isn't a moral evaluation involved when the Law of Attraction is at play. I feel the need to highlight that as I have experienced — both with myself and many others I have spoken with — that we have a tendency to view the universe as a judgemental force that is always deciding who has earned to receive something good, and who hasn't.

In my opinion, this is once again the ego that's at play, by putting the new wisdom about the Law of Attraction, which has come to Earth in recent years, into the old understanding with judgement and verdicts. It is very difficult for the ego to imagine that you don't have to do something to deserve good things, because that has been the foundational premise for the ego's way of being in the world. So, to imagine that the universe is neutral, and that what we receive of good and bad purely stems from universal laws, and that we on top of that have a big influence on how we use it, is a very foreign concept for the ego.

This is naturally thoroughly supported by the religious dogmas that we are all sinners with a range of evil and dark sides which need to be kept in control to be worthy of God's mercy. These ideologies are so deeply embedded into our understanding of life that it can require quite the revolt to wake up to the truth on how we all deserve the best, just because we exist. And that it is not a judging God who decides what we attract and experience, but something we ourselves play a big part in. Because the divine essence of the creator lives within all of us and Love and abundance is attainable for us all. But it is a truth we have to wake up to, here on the threshold to 5D. As I have touched on in previous chapters, an important part of life in 5D is that we take full responsibility for our own life, and thus also our own creation processes. In other words: *that we become conscious creators.*

Because a lot of unconscious creation has been happening in 3D; both individually and collectively. We have all been trapped in what I call *the little self's circle of creation,* which means that we, from the ego's consciousness, have recreated scenarios at the lower part of the vibrational ladder which flow about in an endless circle.

That is quite simply because we have been unaware of how the Law of Attraction really works, and we have been unaware of how big the influence we have on what we ourselves experience is. Right now we are on our way out of the ego's perception that we are victims of unjust fates, and are moving towards a new understanding where we see ourselves as creators. And to create a better world we have to activate *the higher self's spiral of creation*, which creates scenarios that move us upwards on the vibrational ladder. But before we get in-depth on how the ego and higher self creates, and what kind of shift is taking place in our understanding of the creation processes, let's take a quick look at the basic principles of the Law of Attraction, as that is the foundation of it all.

THE LAW OF ATTRACTION AND VIBRATIONS

The two basic principles of the Law of Attraction, which are the most important to know when we are to understand our creation processes, are: *Everything is Vibration*, and *Same attracts Same*.

The first principle is interesting because it is an area where spiritual and traditional science in recent years have come closer to each other — in true 5D spirit, where we find out that apparent conflicting perceptions actually aren't that different. Today it is agreed that a fundamental condition of everything's existence is that everything and everyone vibrates on a certain frequency that can even be measured. This perception is also the reason for the research into feelings and their frequencies, which the vibrational ladder is based on. And learning about the frequencies in our feelings is inevitable when we have to understand our creation processes and want to become conscious creators. Because our emotional frequency is, overall, our most important magnet of attraction. It is the primary signal that the Law of Attraction reads and responds to because of how strong it is. That is why being able to master your emotional frequency and starting processes which bring you up the vibrational ladder, mean so much. And here, Love and gratitude are some of the most important players as they lie at the very top — as we already touched on in the last chapter.

So, the universe responds to the vibration you send out. And it does so from the other fundamental principle — *Same attracts Same*. The emotional frequency you are filled with, regardless of where on the vibrational ladder you are, is reflected by the universe by sending you more of the same. Not because you "deserve it" or "asked for it" in a moral understanding — but because anything else is simply impossible, according to the principles the Law of Attraction works from. You can view the universe's reflection of your inner state as a big gift. What you attract in outer life shows you the state of your inner universe. Based on that, you can take a conscious stand on whether you are happy and satisfied with what you are experiencing — and if you feel it is all too heavy and difficult, you can start to turn on the buttons that lift your frequency. It can be the buttons of self-Love, self-empathy, honouring your own energy signature, forgiveness, gratitude, and the other buttons this book presents.

I hope that it becomes more apparent why I use the concept *Create As Love* with this explanation. Because the more you are filled with Love's vibration, and thus *are* Love, the more you will attract the high vibrational states and emotions that match the Love vibration you are. That is to say, the ones that lie at the very top of the vibrational ladder alongside Love. It happens entirely automatically and naturally, without you needing to actively do anything — besides nurturing Love within yourself, as the previous chapters were about.

Yet again, I feel the need to warn against letting your ego kidnap the knowledge of how the Law of Attraction works. Because something I have experienced many times — both with myself and others who I have worked with on this and taught the principles of creation to — is that we begin to judge ourselves when we don't attract and create the positive conditions and scenarios for ourselves as we desire. Questions like: *"What have I done wrong now — what is it I don't understand?"* or *"What on Earth is the problem with me?"* are the right hand of the ego when things don't happen the way we want them to. They are questions that a lot of us have fought with in our own mind. And that from time to time have also led to a judgemental approach towards other people who attract undesired scenarios of sickness, loss, poor economy, etc.

It is a very harsh and shallow way to handle the profound wisdom of our creation processes. A way that the soul would never choose. Both because the soul knows how incredibly complicated the shift from 3D's to 5D's consciousness is and how much patience and humility it requires to become a conscious creator. And because the soul knows that there are many deep wounds from this and previous lives emerging to be healed when we begin to lift our vibrations, which can make it look like everything is going wrong. And finally, because the soul knows that there are countless invisible parameters at play in the earthly life between souls and it doesn't make sense to judge ourselves or others for what we experience. The soul loves our human self unconditionally and knows that *all is well* and exactly as it should be. The soul contracts we have made with each other before our incarnation, which I spoke about regarding forgiveness in Chapter 4, is a part of the invisible parameters. These commitments, which build on the soul's profound wish to develop certain qualities, inevitably bring challenges into our life, because some qualities are best developed through suffering.

Regarding illness and physical symptoms, it is important to remind yourself that they are completely natural and necessary elements in the process of ascending. Because each time you reclaim a tiny part of your own Love, the higher vibrations will immediately begin to bring forth and cleanse away the low vibrations stored in your body from old, unloving patterns. And the process rarely, not to say never, happens without a variety of bodily symptoms like pain, tension, dizziness, weight gain, or a regular cold/influenza. It is all a part of the upgrading of your cells, so they match the new vibrations. In addition to this comes bodily reactions that the general rise of vibrations in and around Earth brings. This includes the many energy portals that open up, and the following stream of 5D vibrations to both the planet and our individual bodies. We all carry the memories of our true essence in bones, muscles, organs, DNA, etc., and when these are activated through the 5D stream, a range of physical reactions are released, which in the spiritual world goes under the term ascension-symptoms.

So, to begin creating as Love does not equal a life with constant wind under your wings. You can look at the process of lifting your vibrations from a few words of wisdom that I read many years ago — the source I, unfortunately, do not remember.

If you feel that you are experiencing many challenges, then it is not because you are doing anything wrong, but because you are doing things right.

These are wise words that can hopefully tame your ego's desire to beat yourself and others up when challenges and pain arise on the way up the vibrational ladder. And they hopefully instead awake the soul's Love and compassion. Because the way you meet yourself in the challenges you encounter is a much better way to gauge how your ascension process is going, rather than what your actual state is like. And that way is really about whether it is your ego or higher self that you allow to control the process. Whether what you experience makes you react with fear and panic from your little self, or respond with Love and trust from your higher self. Let's look closer at those two parts of you and the creation processes they each enact.

Your Ego and Higher Self — and Creation

To be able to place your higher self into the driver's seat in your ascension process, you must begin to think of yourself as a multidimensional being. In 3D, most of us have identified with the ego — or the little self. We have viewed ourselves and others solely as the physical beings we are here on Earth, with the limits of time and space it entails. The reason for that is, of course, that the veil between life on Earth and the spiritual levels — and thus the spiritual part of ourselves — has been so thick and impenetrable, as I have touched on earlier.

But in recent years, as the vibrations on Earth have notably risen and the veil has gotten thinner, a significant awareness about the spiritual aspects of our identities has appeared. If we, i.e., look at the use of the word *soul* on the Internet and social media, I have registered a remarkable rise. And the way we use and view the term *soul* today is not in a mystical and unreachable state that is only accessible to certain enlightened meditation nerds, as it was back in the "old days". We use it much more as an accessible part of us that we can connect with daily for help through specific methods and practices that put the ego on standby. Which this book is one of many examples of. The awareness that we are much more than our little self, as we have previously identified with, and that we have a higher self that is not limited by time and space and, because of that, is in better touch with the truth about us and life, has evolved significantly during the vibrational rise on Earth. And it is that higher self you need to awake to as you move up the vibrational ladder to become one with Love's vibration, and thus begin to create as Love.

But let's just look at how you keep an eye on whether the ego's circle of creation is active in your life. Because only by knowing how it works can you — lovingly but assertively — ensure that you don't unknowingly hold onto it. It has been the primary process of creation for many, many years in 3D, and it thrives in the sub-conscious worlds within each of us. So, there is good reason to be awake and aware of what type of creation you are practicing. Another thing on the ego's circle of creation and the beliefs that lie behind it to be aware of, is that it naturally also lives on in the collective field. So you constantly meet it through other people, the media, and politician's interpretations of what is happening in the world. And the ego's consciousness has its way of overriding the higher self's consciousness when it can get away with it. It all comes from the fear of change and the we-know-what-we-have-but-not-what-we-get philo-sophy that the ego's view on life is based on.

Comments like *"It doesn't work, you can probably see that it never has,"* *"How about that thing that is happening in the world right now?"* *"You have no understanding of what the people affected are going through,"* and *"I don't believe that, because humans are fundamentally power-hungry,"* are completely normal to encounter when you begin to look at what is happening in the world and your life from your higher self's perspective and mention it to others. And it is completely natural because, as long as we are in the ego's circle of creation, the world really does *look* the way it does from the little self's perspective. Therefore, it is often not a good idea to partake in discussions about whether it can be true that we can create something better and more loving than what has appeared in 3D for millennia. Or about whether to lift your own vibration can change both your life and the world around you, because we are all connected and *same attracts same.* Those types of discussions can easily create unloving and hostile relationships — and then we will have done more harm than good.

So, my recommendation is that you primarily exercise connecting to your higher self when you are alone, or with others who also have their eyes set on another and bigger reality that we can tap into. If you feel called to do so, you can, every now and then, suggest to the sceptics around you a difference they can make in their own lives (without entering a discussion) if they are not content. With sincere respect for their truth to be just as true as your truth is to you — and that none of us really know the full truth. But sometimes, it can be really illuminating and eye-opening to hear others' truth.

same

attracts

same

The COVID-19 Scenario as an Example of Creation

Let us now take a look at how the ego's circle of creation works. The vibrational ladder is our basis — which you can see a diagram of in Chapter 4. Let's say that your little self primarily finds itself around the steps in the middle — where the feelings of being overwhelmed, worried, disappointed, doubtful, frustrated, irritated, impatient, pessimistic, and bored exist. It is a place where many of us ended up during the challenging time of COVID-19 and the many restrictions following that.

The exchange that is taking place between you and the universe when you find yourself there is then an exchange where you radiate the frequency of the feelings mentioned, and where you then receive something that matches the same frequency. Your feelings are perhaps created by thinking about how hopeless it all is, how dangerous it can become, and whether or not a better world will ever be on the way. Or — if you weren't or aren't currently scared of the virus and are one of those who found or find it now to be a bit exaggerated — you might be thinking about how annoying it was or is to hear about that virus all the time, how frustrated you were or are with everyone who is shocked by fear, and how much you needed or need your freedom back. All of these thoughts create feelings which lie just at the middle of the ladder.

When that is the frequency you project and the one you receive, this reaffirms the thoughts and beliefs in the little self's mind. Your feelings of hopelessness, anxiety about

COVID-19, doubt, irritation, frustration, and impatience are empowered because the universe reflects them, so you can see what you are doing. And in the ego's consciousness, the reflection works as a confirmation that it is correct: *"You see? It is exactly like I said and thought — that thing that just happened confirms it."* The ego does not think: *"Alright, that is what I have created; I think I am going to change that,"* because the ego does not view itself as a creator, but instead as a victim of some — often unfair and dangerous — incident. So, the ego interprets the loving reflection of its own thoughts and feelings that the universe presents, as yet another piece of evidence that the fear-scenarios it believed in were true. In that way, the little self goes round and round in a circle of creation where the frequency that is sent is reflected and affirmed by the universe, whereafter it radiates more of the same type, which will then again be reflected and affirmed. Thus, the little self is constantly recreating scenarios that look the same frequency-wise.

This circle is active both individually for each of us and collectively as a society. And with COVID-19, it was easy to see that the story about how we are all innocent victims of a foreign and potentially lethal virus was being nurtured quite a bit in the public eye. There weren't many voices that spoke on how we know that by changing our thoughts about it all, thus our feelings, and thus our frequency can alter the development of the situation. There was not much talk about how important it is to let the individual and collective higher self control how we are handling the situation. We were also not hearing many express the more grounded view, which is that we — including politicians, the media, and health workers — more than anything in the world should avoid inducing fear in ourselves, because the fear itself weakens our immune system and makes us sick. It is the age-old story about how the body, if it is filled with fear and stress because it thinks it's about to be killed by a tiger, shuts down all other bodily functions, including the immune system and other life-giving processes. The few that dared to express these and similar views in this particular time were quickly publicly shamed — overruled by the collective little self, as I mentioned earlier, because the time still hasn't come for the collective higher self to take care of the COVID-19 situation.

So, in this situation, we have seen a lot of creation from the little self's fear in the public space, which I see as the last round of 3D consciousness in full flow. Shown before our eyes and reflected by the loving universe, allowing us to see what we are doing. And we can then decide if we want to continue down that road. Maybe one of the biggest gifts the new Coronavirus has to offer is exactly that — to wake up the higher self in each and every one of us to the bigger truth about our existence. That we have so much power and strength to both resist and get through an infection of the actual virus when we let go of the fear and let Love, trust, and gratitude take the wheel. And that we, with our inherent power to create, have a big influence on which direction the situation is headed. Even though that consciousness is not present in the public space at this moment, you can still work towards it in your own system. When you begin to move up the vibrational ladder — through self-Love, self-empathy, forgiveness, gratitude, and the other tools you have received in this book — you rise above the ego's circle of creation and into what I call the higher self's spiral of creation. You might climb the ladder one step at a time — up to hope and satisfaction because you start searching for the gift of the situation, and practise gratitude for the new possibilities the COVID-19 situation *also* brought with it.

And after that, you might — slowly but surely — move further up until the point where you arrive at the top step where Love resides. Because to begin creating from the higher self is precisely like an upwards spiral where the energy from one step, like hope and satisfaction, automatically lifts you to the next step in a self-reinforcing process — if you keep your focus on it, that is. A few rollercoaster trips downwards can, of course, happen every now and then, as I mentioned previously. But when you enter the higher self's spiral of creation, you lift your fundamental frequency, which means that your rollercoaster trips become shorter, and you can get back up quite quickly, like a cork that neither wants to nor is able to stay underwater for very long. And then you are well underway to create from Love's vibration. Let's take a closer look at what is awaiting you.

Your Journey Up the Vibrational Ladder

As I touched on earlier, *to create as Love* does not guarantee a life free of suffering. But, as I have already mentioned, it still makes a huge change in your experience of being in the world if your creation processes come from the top part of the vibrational ladder — compared to coming from the lower part. The huge difference is whether you manage to turn the suffering and challenges into something positive that brings your frequency back up again — or if you let them get a hold of you in a way where your frequency stays low. Note: I don't recommend that you force yourself to "be positive" without first meeting the difficult feelings with Love and empathy — but more so that you, by meeting the difficult feelings with Love and empathy, heal your inner wounds so your positive stance and joy of life come from within and your frequency therefore automatically rises.

And remember: It is many thousand year old codes that we are in the middle of transforming in this gigantic shift that is happening. So, be patient with yourself and make sure to also make room for your little self on your journey up the vibrational ladder. Be the loving, com-passionate parent that meets the little self's fear, anger, and powerlessness as you would meet a child filled with — in the adult's eyes — an irrational fear. Here you would probably never say: *"No, stop that right now. We can't take care of that; it doesn't make any sense!"* Instead, you'd explain to the child that there is nothing to be afraid of, that you can see that they are scared, and that you will take care of them. This is how, with Love and empathy, I would recommend for your higher self to take care of your little self on your journey of lifting your frequency.

When you begin to move up the vibrational ladder, pay attention to what is happening with your creation processes. Can you register a more easy-going exchange with the universe of high vibrating states of being? Do you feel a larger sense of lightness, more optimism, and hope in the entirety of your system? Do you become better at finding gifts in your challenges and being grateful for the development it offers you? Is there less darkness, resistance, and inertia in your life and your creation processes than before? Do you begin to attract different people, situations, and conditions which match you and your needs/desires/values/dreams more? I think you will be able to register some of the things mentioned above because, once we lift our frequency and begin to create from a higher stage on the vibrational ladder, we begin to attract something that mirrors the lighter and more positive aspects of ourselves. In 3D, there were so many sides of ourselves that were still hidden in the shadow. Because of that we needed to have those sides of us still in the dark be reflected by other people and challenging situations, so we could notice them, integrate them, and heal them. That is why we have had a tendency to attract opposites and things that created resistance in 3D — which we can call work-aspects — which have brought us through our process of discovering all parts of ourselves.

In 5D, when we achieve a higher frequency, we will have discovered and integrated more of the shadow-parts that were previously living in the dark and unknown. There are fewer of them, and that is why our co-creation with the universe typically entails a reflection of the lighter parts of us. We will experience more lightness and ease, and less darkness and inertia in our processes of creation. So, I will strongly encourage you to keep an eye on that development. It is important to register, feel, and appreciate the positive changes that happen — both within you and in what the universe sends your way as a reflection of your higher vibrations. That awareness is exactly where you get nourishment and strength to continue with your process — even when you slide down every now and then. The more you anchor and embody your high vibrational feelings — through enjoying them, taking deep breaths, and consciously connecting to the parts of the body where they reside — the more you can be sure that your cork-mechanism works and will instinctively bring you up again. Your body is unbelievably clever and your best friend on the journey up the ladder. When it has felt how it is to live in and with the higher vibrations, it will do everything it can to get you back to that state.

Another thing I will encourage you to pay attention to is whether your processes of creation begin to happen more from the inside-out rather than outside-in. By that, I mean if you can recognise the inner-steered way of being in the world — as I touched on earlier in the book. That is to say that your impulses, actions, and decisions come from the inside, through your GPS, instead of the outer-steered way where they come in the shape of other people's takes and opinions, or the traditional societal norms about what you should do and what is right, good, clever, reasonable, and realistic to do. We can also phrase it as to whether they mostly come from the heart instead of the brain. Because very often, the journey up the ladder means a larger belief and trust in your own inner impulses, and more courage to act upon them and stand firmly in your own light and truth. And it isn't that odd because the destination you are on your way towards is your own heart, where Love resides at the top of the ladder. So, the journey up the vibrational ladder will often feel like a journey out of the brain and into the heart. Away from your own and others' old expectations and demands of you, and into your most profound needs/desires/values/dreams.

We can also say it like this: Where the creation processes in 3D have been driven by the masculine energy — conceive, write goals, make plans and strategies, consider pros and cons, put things into work based on what seems sensible and rational — we in 5D begin to bring in the feminine energy as the basis for our creation processes. The heart's feminine wisdom, which speaks to us through our needs/desires/values/dreams, becomes the very foundation for the things we set into action, and the masculine energy's finest task is to put the inspiration from the feminine wisdom into practise. It is a different form of creation than what we are familiar with. It rests on the balance and equal collaboration between the masculine and the feminine, as I touched on in Chapter 3. And it is another aspect of 5D's interpretation of creation as a process that happens from the inside-out.

This Book as an Example of 5D Creation

As an example of all of this, I can mention my process of writing this book. It is the first crystal clear sign in my life that creation from the inside-out happens much faster and easier than the old type of creation. With well-developed proactivity, I have worked and produced a lot in 3D and certainly made many good things happen. But I have never before experienced the creation process unfolding with such ease and the concrete creations manifesting themselves so quickly as with this book. However, I *have* actually experienced this in my artistic work with songwriting — which I will get back to in a bit.

I got the urge to write this book in August of 2020 during a meditation session. It stood with such clarity before me and the title so vividly that it was impossible to avoid, unless I were to forcefully choose to ignore my inner voice. And I, fortunately, don't do that anymore, even if I not only a moment before that meditation have had the thought that I should write a book titled *Love in the 5th Dimension*. After digesting it for a month, I began to write in September based on some notes and bullet points about the content that had come to me in spurts throughout the month that had passed. In the beginning of November, the book was almost done. That is a very short timeframe to write a book. And several times during the process, I thought of the mantra *the universe loves speed*, which is to be understood in the way that, when we quickly and without the brain's reservations act on the insight we receive from the heart, it is supported in virtuous ways by the universe. There has been free flow and wind under my wings all the way during this process of creation.

I view the flow as an example of how I have let my inner feminine wisdom lead the way, putting my masculine vigour entirely to the feminine's service. That's what we can call *inspired action*, where the masculine's actions are inspired by the feminine's wisdom. I set aside time to write pretty much every day (thanks, Corona) and opened myself to what was to come. And the content came effortlessly in a stream of creation without any blockage. I never, at any point, experienced it as a difficult process. It was often that I, in those two months, thought and said to myself: *"This book is already written — I just have to open myself to it,"* because that is how it truly felt. Whether it is my higher self that was writing through my earthly self or other spiritual beings were at play, I simply do not know. I only know that the book has been created in collaboration with a consciousness larger than my earthly consciousness. A consciousness that can see the connections and opportunities my earthbound self can't. I noticed — and enjoyed — throughout it all that almost all of the experiences and accumulated knowledge from my entire life have contributed to the book. Here is a selection of the most important ones:

- My childhood in the '60s with my parents' upbringing as an influence, and the twisted love and trauma it caused.

- My youth in the '70s, and my strong awareness of and participation in the up-coming of the feminine energy.
- My education as a magister and the experience I have gotten from that, amongst others, to create written products.
- My private life and my process in untangling myself from the twisted love from co-dependency and over-responsibility, to free and authentic. And from first-love-others to first-love-self.
- My understanding of what true Love and compassion is in that regard.
- My spiritual passion through the last twenty-five years where I have studied the paradigm shift and its meaning for our lives on Earth, amongst others through different mystery schools.
- My spiritual work since 2007 with my company *Empower You* where I develop and hold courses (in Danish) and presentations on empowerment — how we lift our vibrations and use the Law of Attraction in the creation of our lives.
- My teaching over many years in non-violent/empathic communication (Marshall Rosenberg), on which I wrote my first book.

Although I naturally embodied the wisdom and insight as expressed in this book, my earthbound consciousness would not have been able to figure out, over a period of two months, how all of the dots could be connected in a comprehensive and meaningful way to others. I would have faced way too many considerations, speculations, censorships, reflections, and what-if's — all of which would have stopped the process. But by opening myself to the process and trusting what has been coming through, everything I embody has become part of the book. You could say that the book, in a way, has become a direct extension of me and my unique energy signature. And that is the distinguishable sign of the creation we will experience in 5D — that *our creations are as we are.*

Earlier, I wrote that my artistic work as a songwriter has always felt like this trouble-free inside-out creation process. When I create my *empowering songs for the soul,* they come to me effortlessly and with ease. Out of the blue when I am walking, lying on the beach, or in other situations where I am not doing anything. I have always intuitively known that I should let that process happen exactly as it wants to, without censorship and over-thinking, and with a deep respect for the creations that come through. And when I have received a song from my open feminine channel, I use my masculine energy to complete, record, produce, and release it. So really, my artistic identity should be on the list above, too, as it has also been a big part of the making of this book. But then, instead, it got its own paragraph.

And it is an important paragraph because it might just be precisely from the artistic world that we can get inspiration and a deeper understanding of our creation processes in 5D. Since we all contain the essence of the creator within us, we are in that regard all artists that constantly create, no matter if we are aware of it or not. So, while working to cultivate our creation processes and becoming conscious creators, we can be inspired by the artists' creative processes, which in the future will, without doubt, be much more valued and respected than what we have experienced in 3D. Here I want to guide your attention towards a book I was very inspired by as a songwriter many years ago: *The Artist's Way* by Julia Cameron. It is structured like a twelve-week course you take at home for and with yourself, and is designed to open up your creativity in the artist's way. I highly recommend it if you want to kickstart just that.

But let us now take a look at how you can empower your inner artist and cultivate your creation processes without reading more books, but through the exercises and tips below.

EXERCISES & TIPS

In this section you will receive different tips to elevate your vibrations, cultivate your send-and-receive station, and give energy to and nourish your deepest dreams so they quickly manifest. They are three very different methods that each work on separate levels, but they all strengthen your ability to attract high vibrating states.

You can use the first exercise in your everyday life when you sense your vibrations falling and feel yourself getting caught in a heavy state of being; like rage, powerlessness, sorrow, or abandonment. It will help you lift your vibration right here and now.

The following two exercises work on a more long-term basis. One is a meditative exercise that attunes and cultivates your send-and-receive station, and thus your exchange with the universe. By elevating the vibrations in what you are radiating to the universe, you support insuring that what the universe is sending you is also of high vibrations.

The other long-term exercise is a daily practice of writing in your future diary to let your inner dreams take shape and become solid images and experiences. This will help your dreams manifest in your life easier and quicker.

EXERCISE 10
Three Tips
to Elevate Your Vibrations

This is a method to elevate your vibrations right here and now when you feel the need for it. There are three different tips that you can use as much and however you want, when you wish. None of these three tips are better than the other. Only you know what works best for you.

The First Tip: Think About Someone You Love

A very simple way to elevate your vibrations is by *thinking of someone you love.* It can be your old grandmother, your favourite teacher from school, a child, a pet, your guardian angel, Virgin Mary, Mother Earth — or, of course, your partner.

When you choose who you want to embrace with loving thoughts, there must be an *uncomplicated* love-relation between you and the person. This is why children, pets, and angels are good for this practice, while there is often something a bit complicated in our love-relations to other adults. So, it is important that you have as much unconditional Love for the person you are thinking about as possible.

The Second Tip: Think of Something You Are Grateful For

Another simple way of lifting your vibrations is by focusing on something you are grateful for. No matter if you are in a difficult or challenging situation, you will always — as you know from Chapter 4 — be able to find something you are grateful for. Maybe not relating to the difficult situation, but from other aspects of your life.

The Third Tip: Choose Affirmations That Bring You Relief

The last tip is to choose thoughts that give you relief. Just like Love and gratitude, relief is a high vibrating feeling. Any thoughts/affirmations that bring you a deep and warm physical sensation of relief works. The feeling of relief often appears with a spontaneous inhale the body takes for itself. Experiment with different thoughts and see if you can achieve this effect.

This is how you use all of the three tips:

Close your eyes, think of the person you love/ what you are grateful for/the affirmation that brings you relief. Take a few deep breaths and *feel* the Love, gratitude, and relief fill you up. The more physical your feelings are, the better. The moment you sense your feelings in the body, your frequency has risen.

Expand your experience of Love/gratitude/ relief by taking in *all* of the sensations: See, feel, listen, taste, smell — the more senses you open when you let yourself be full of the high vibrating feelings, the better they work on your frequency as you make the feeling even more physical. ENJOY the feeling. Indulge in it and breathe it deeply in and out of your lungs, preferably with your mouth open to activate the energy in the body.

Take a final deep breath, open your eyes, and feel your vibration. Can you sense that it has risen? That what was weighing on you is lighter now? Perhaps it hasn't fully disappeared, but it takes up less space than it did before? If you can sense the change, then carry on with your day — now with more of the new, lighter vibration. If not, do the exercise again — maybe a bit later in the day. Practice makes perfect.

Note: The three tips can, of course, be combined in different ways. It might be that you find someone or something to think of that fills you with Love, gratitude, and relief all at the same time. Your imagination is the limit.

EXERCISE 11

Attuning Your
Send-and-Receive Station

This is a meditative exercise where you attune your send-and-receive station and refine the exchange you have with the universe.

This is how you do it:
Sit, lay down, or stand in a quiet place where you won't be disturbed. Take a few deep breaths and become completely present in your body. Let your system calm down.

Now begin to inhale and exhale from the heart. Imagine that there is a nose in the heart area, from where the breathing happens. Caress your heart area with the air in your breath; soft and compassionate. Continue until you feel that you rest calmly and worry-free in your heart.

Now, imagine your body as your send-and-receive station exactly as you want it to be. It might be a tree, a flower, a crystal, a lit-up bubble, a mountain, a radio tower, or something else. The image might change each time you do the exercise.

Regardless of what you imagine, expand your send-and-receive station to contain colours, shapes, sounds, scents …

How do you look, how do you smell, what colours do you contain, what shape do you have, are you transparent or opaque in structure, are you soft or hard, do you have a sound …? Regardless of how you imagine yourself, expand your experience with all of the nuances you can think of and sense yourself through all of your senses.

Now move your attention back towards the heart area, inhale and exhale through the heart. When you inhale, imagine that you are inhaling all of the universe surrounding you from the front, back, and sides of the heart area. And when you exhale, imagine your breath reaching all of the universe, again from all sides.

Feel your connection and exchange with the universe in your send-and-receive station, which centres in the heart like this. Sit, lie, or stand as long as you want during this exchange.

Expansion — To Breathe in Eights

When you are comfortable with the exercise, you can begin to expand your breath, so it happens in eights.

Up/down:

- As you inhale, you guide the consciousness in an arc from the heart and behind the body, over the head, and down in front of the body to land in the heart again.

- Pause briefly.
- As you exhale, you guide the consciousness in an arc from the heart behind the body and down below the feet, and up in front of the body to land in the heart again.
- Pause briefly.
- When you have done this a couple of times, you can leave out the pauses and let the breath flow freely.

After this, you might add ...

Right-left:

- Imagine (or physically do it) your arms stretched out horizontally.
- As you inhale, you guide the consciousness in an arc from the heart and horizontally behind the right arm, around the hand, and back in front of the arm to land in the heart again.
- As you exhale, you guide the consciousness in an arc from the heart and horizontally behind the left arm, around the hand, and back in front of the arm to land back in the heart again.

To breathe in eights helps to make your exchange with the universe organic and fluid. You strengthen your connection with the universe and elevate your experience so that there is no separation, but that your creation processes and the universe come together and co-create in a free flow.

Use all of the elements, including the expansions, from this exercise as it suits you. You don't need to use all of the elements each time, but can pick and choose as you wish.

EXERCISE 12

Future Diary

This daily exercise will help you to nourish your most profound dreams. An important part of manifesting your dreams is to bring yourself into a state where you can sense how it feels when you experience them. At the same time, it gives direction and focuses on your inspired actions, so they can support your heart's desires.

This is how you do it:
You write about your life as *you want it to take shape.*

You write in the present as if the dreams have already come true.

Don't use words such as: When, if, maybe, I dream of, I would like to …

Instead write: I do … I feel … I am … I say …

Divide your life into different sections and write about each area separately:

- Love life
- Economy
- Work
- Health
- Residence
- Friends
- …

I would recommend that you start by picking one area to write about for a month. Then you have the best possibility of seeing what the practice does to you and which results you achieve.

You can set aside time every day as it suits you — from five-ten minutes, half an hour, or more. Give yourself as much time as you need to emotionally enter your future universe and "forget time and space" for a while. The more excitement, enthusiasm, joy, and optimism you can create in your whole system through this writing practice, the stronger and higher the vibrating impulses will be that you send into the universe — and the more you ensure that things will happen.

And lastly: Remember to notice when your dreams and wishes actually come true. We often don't notice when the things we have desired become part of our lives, because we have elevated our vibrations so much that it now just feels natural and has become second nature in our lives. Reading back in your future diary might help remind you of where you were previously and in which ways you have evolved.

When you notice these types of miracles, then appreciate yourself for creating them and celebrate that you have become a more conscious and powerful creator.

CHAPTER 6

Love in the 5th Dimension

On Everything's Connectedness

I hope you aren't overwhelmed by the many ways back to Love, and thus yourself, that I have presented in the previous chapters. If it feels impossible to integrate all these techniques into your way of being in this world, I have got good news for you — it is all actually deeply connected and braided together.

And what do I mean by that? I mean that when you first begin to turn one of the buttons, the others will automatically follow. Let me try to give an example with self-Love as the basis, the theme of Chapter 2. This is the most important button, as loving yourself is the key to opening up for your connection with the infinite source of Love, from where Love flows through you and the ones you are close to. So, when you begin to meet and treat yourself more lovingly and empathetically — i.e., through the exercises at the end of Chapter 2 — it will automatically unlock the ways I have presented in the other chapters. Because when your Love for yourself becomes an active vibration within you, you won't be able to avoid doing what Chapter 3 is all about — that is, to be true to yourself and the messages you receive from your soul through your inner GPS. And you will then instinctively honour and cherish your unique energy signature and speak from the heart. Because when you love yourself, you begin to value your own energy so much that to not be true to yourself and listen to your inner GPS — regardless of what anyone else thinks — will be a very foreign concept to you. On top of that, you will be able to set healthy boundaries peacefully, because you no longer discuss with yourself whether or not you have the right to do so. Deep within your heart, you know that you, of course, do.

In the same way, the forgiveness of both yourself and others, as we touched on in Chapter 4, will naturally proceed from your increased self-Love. Because all of the rage, grief, grudges, bitterness, and guilt of what happened in the past, which you carry, comes from your experience of not being loved and appreciated. And when you finally give yourself that Love and appreciation — plan A, as you might remember — the wound that was kept open is healed, and you will be able to forgive and set yourself and others free from what has happened in your life. From here, gratitude follows, something we also spoke about in Chapter 4. When you realise that you and everyone else have played roles in each other's lives that you decided on at soul level, inner gratitude for what the other souls have agreed to contribute will automatically emerge. And when you then search for the gift and notice the unique opportunities for evolvement that you have given to each other, your eyes will open up to even more of the magical and miraculous adventures that life is — and then you will become even more grateful. Finally, strengthening your Love for yourself will naturally bring you up the vibrational ladder, so you — without doing anything else than meeting yourself with more

Love and empathy — set creation processes into action, which brings even more Love as we touched on in Chapter 5.

That is how all the paths to Love intuitively overlap and nicely connect. You don't necessarily have to start to consciously practise all of the methods this book presents, but trust that when you start fiddling with one button, the others will follow. So, *if* you feel overwhelmed, I hope these examples provide you with a more manageable picture of it all.

I want to encourage you to begin trying the one or two exercises that speak to you the most and let them become part of your everyday life for a little while. Pay attention to what good things they bring along. Most of all, I want to encourage you to keep an open eye on whether your vibrational level is moving — and whether it is on the way up or down the vibrational ladder. Because it is important to be aware that both directions are self-reinforcing — both the spiral down to the fear at the bottom, and the spiral up towards the Love at the top. You are the one to decide that, from now on, you are on the upwards ascension spiral — and to bring that decision to fruition you can use any of the exercises in this book.

I think that it is this self-reinforcing mechanism Jesus wanted to make us aware of when he, as written in the Gospel of Matthew, 13:12, said: *"Whoever has will be given more, and they will have an abundance,"* — a phrase we in many ways have struggled to fit in with the other messages Jesus came with. But perhaps he was really trying to shine a light on the importance of taking responsibility for our vibrations and to open our eyes to the self-reinforcing process that Love generates. That way, we get into an exchange with the universe that brings us abundance. That is at least my humble interpretation of his words.

Unity Consciousness

That all the paths you have encountered in this book are in this way connected resonates with the bigger truth of everything's connectivity, which is a central aspect of the 5D consciousness. We are on a path away from the ego's perception that we and everything are separate from each other, which has created seemingly in-compatible polarisations. This path leads us towards the soul's awareness that we and everything are connected, thus creating a higher level called positive polarisation. It goes for the different ways to Love, which are different but at the same time connected and in no way each other's opposites.

But it also goes for all other aspects of life, hereunder the different parts you consist of. In this book, we have touched on some of those parts, i.e., the brain-heart aspect that we in 3D have viewed as separate parts that work differently and in opposite ways. In 5D's conscious-ness of oneness, the two ways aren't necessarily opposites. We have to get used to the heart and mind melting together and working as one consciousness, which some call *the heartmind* — a state of consciousness where there is no separation between what the mind and heart desires. We often view the mind as the human part of us, and the heart as the divine part. When we are in 5D's unity consciousness, we will experience the two merge.

Another seemingly polarised aspect we have touched on in this book is the feminine-masculine aspect. You might remember from Chapter 3 that we are heading towards a time where the feminine and masculine will enter an equal and fruitful coalition, and all individuals will begin developing their opposite gender's qualities. That means, in part, that it will soften up the stark difference between men and women which we have experienced in 3D. This evolvement away from stark polarisations and towards the unity of the masculine and the feminine is already visible in today's society, i.e., through women's natural focus on education and careers, and young men's empathetic fatherhood. You can also expect the merging of the masculine and the feminine to happen within yourself. As I touched on in Chapter 5, the future's creation and way of making decisions and choices comes from a harmonious partnership between your masculine and feminine sides, where your masculine I's most important task is to act on what comes from your feminine I's wisdom and insight. The biggest challenge for most of us is not to feel what the soul whispers to us through the feminine channel — our feelings and the inner GPS. No, the biggest challenge is to have the courage to honour and act on what comes from within. This challenge becomes easier to handle in a natural and intuitive way the more we move up the vibrational ladder and connect ourselves to the unity consciousness in 5D.

One last aspect of the unity consciousness I want to talk about is how each time you make a change in your vibration, it affects the whole. This is an important aspect to be aware of — especially for you who is fighting with the egoism-devil trying to convince you that you aren't allowed to be that concerned about yourself. And that all the focus on your own Love vibration and fulfilling your own needs/desires/values/dreams, will only make you self-obsessed and prevent you from loving others. My experience is that knowing the truth about how our individual healing work has a healing effect on the collective field can be a very welcome friend to have within reach when it comes to neutralising this devil. The thing is that since we are all connected, every time you untangle a part of your twisted love by meeting yourself with unconditional Love and empathy, it will affect the whole. Every time you step up on the ladder, the vibration of the collective field is elevated. Every time you forgive and show gratitude, a release of the ego's perception of being a victim of an unfair fate happens to the collective human consciousness. And every time your exchange with the universe results in you creating a more positive and higher vibrating scenario for yourself, you create a more positive scenario in the field of possibilities that, again, affects the whole.

And all of this doesn't *just* happen because it is nice and uplifting for others to be with a happier, more loving, free, grateful, and aware creative version of you — which is an evident positive effect in itself. But it also happens because everything is vibrational and every little lift in your frequency automatically lifts the entire universe's frequency. It sounds big, and it is. Even if we can't see it with our naked eyes, we will, with our new united consciousness, begin to understand and integrate how powerful we are and how much our Love vibration means. It is something I have heard time after time from the spiritual side throughout the years. When there, i.e., has been a huge natural disaster, lots of messages have come to Earth that want to tell us what an incredible effect our compassion has had on the collective field. I have often heard phrases like: *"If you could only see all the light your compassionate thoughts create, you would cheer,"* and several times it has even been clarified that some natural disasters happen exactly to activate humanity's compassion, because it's enormous healing ability is precisely what Mother Earth needs.

It is something that has taken me many years to understand. That I should have such a big role in the huge process of healing that is taking place on Earth in these years — and that my individual healing of personal trauma at the same time heals the trauma that Mother Earth has had to take on in the long age of 3D — was more than what my separation-consciousness was able to process. When I began to seriously study the energy shift around twenty years ago, I thought, like

*every little lift
in your
frequency
automatically
lifts the entire
universe's
frequency*

many others at the time, that the shift would solely come externally through the high vibrational inflow of 5D energy to Earth. And that the increased Love vibration would effortlessly dissolve 3D's unloving and limited programmes, and bring healing, solution, and ease to all of the globe's citizens instead. But it turned out not to be that way. Today, there is no doubt in my mind that Mother Earth's healing comes through each and every individual — through our conscious integration of 5D's Love vibration and thus the healing of our own system. The new energy offers unique opportunities for pro-found transformation and healing, but we have to choose the path on our own. When we make that choice, the whole universe will cheer, and we will receive all of the help and support we need. *God helps the one who helps themselves.*

The connection between mine, yours, and Mother Earth's healing process is expressed beautifully by Louise Hay in her final book *Trust Life*. It is a book with affirmations for each day, year-round, which I highly recommend for your daily Love-supplement. She sums the topic about this interconnectedness up in a simple yet profound way:

> *"As we each practice Unconditional Love of ourselves and others, the entire planet will heal."*

I hope this wisdom helps strengthen your belief that your work in upgrading your self-Love truly means something, not just for you but to the whole that you are an inseparable part of. And I am sure that you, while elevating your vibration and getting closer to a state where Love vibrates with stability in your heart and body, more and more will feel one with everything and everyone.

Relationships in 5D

Throughout this book, I have touched on how increasing your ability to love yourself automatically means that you have more Love to give to others and at the same time attracts more loving and empathetic people. But as this is a book about Love, and as we most commonly relate Love with something exchanged between people, let me then still say a few words on Love in relationships. Through my own process, and from other people I have worked with, I know there is a sense of doubt that many people clash with in the process of strengthening their self-Love. That's the doubt about whether we are even able to love others if we start to love, respect, honour, and cherish ourselves as this book encourages — or if we become too self-sufficient. There is also a doubt and confusion on whether Love between two people can even exist if there isn't a sort of inherent dependency. Can two free and independent people who love themselves and stand in their own light even find meaning in an intimate relationship with each other?

It is a natural and understandable doubt seen in the light of 3D's twisted love that has made us believe that Love and dependency are connected. My experience is that Love in a close relationship not only becomes easier but also deeper the more the parties become more self-contained and reclaim their own Love and light. This goes for romantic relationships, parent-child relationships, and friendships. When we each rest securely in our hearts and are true to our own unique energy signature, the relationship is no longer anchored in healing each other's wounds, filling each other's holes or saving each other's lives. As we have taken responsibility for ourselves, it becomes about supplementing each other's energy on a higher level. My old master Kuthumi-Agrippa, who I have talked about before, in his lectures at the mystery school often used to say that we are in the middle of moving from a kind of Love where we *fall in love*, to a kind of Love where *we rise in love*. In 3D, we have extensively used close relationships to mirror our shadow sides and trauma. By seeing them in our partner or other people close to us, we have been able to spot them and integrate them — if we have handled the mirroring wisely and taken full responsibility for our shadow sides, that is. These mirroring patterns could make the Love activate a *fall* down the vibrational ladder in 3D.

In 5D's unity consciousness, we have integrated most of our dark and heavy sides and healed most of our trauma. This means that there are fairly few shadows and wounds we need to mirror. The people and relationships we attract in 5D are thus not necessarily our opposites as we know from 3D. When our foundational frequency begins to find itself at the top of the vibrational ladder, we attract more people and relations that match the higher aspects of us — our self-Love and our light, authenticity, strength, and trust. Thus Love in 5D is a kind of Love that activates a *rise* and brings the individuals up in vibration.

As you have probably already put together, there are, in my experience, only good things to say about the evolvement that happens in our close, loving relationships when we each move home in ourselves and reclaim Love as this book guides you to. However, my experience from the development of my own romantic relationship is that it is not Love without challenges that awaits us in 5D. There are still dis-crepancies and discussions on different ways to handle the relationship and other problematic aspects. But when both parties have met themselves on such a deep level that the quest of reclaiming Love requires, less unaware self-projection happens in the relationship — which makes a big difference. Each individual takes responsibility for themselves and becomes clearer and more authentic on a level I most certainly didn't experience when I was in a dependency-influenced relationship in 3D.

That means that in the discussions and discrepancies that occur, each part speaks and acts from their connection with their inner GPS and thus their own needs/desires/ values/dreams. That is a determining factor because our needs/desires/values/dreams will always find a way to come through because they are such strong drivers for us. And if we aren't true to ourselves and aren't able to express ourselves directly about them — as you saw some simple examples on how to do so in Chapter 3 — they will lash out in different ways. I.e., through indirect and manipulative communication where we aren't talking about what is really at stake (our needs/desires/values/ dreams), but about what is wrong with the other person that we feel is standing in the way of what we want. Even though it is really ourselves standing in the way. And then the discussions become barren and the relationship draining. On that note, it is worth paying attention to just how closely Love and honesty are intertwined. Because having the courage to be completely honest about my most inner needs/desires/values/dreams is perhaps how I can show my partner the truest Love. My authenticity and honesty means that he doesn't doubt where I stand, and then doesn't need to start a draining guessing competition about why I am reacting the way I am. But even more so, being true to myself means that I naturally give him the space to be true to himself, too. And to listen to myself and my inner needs/desires/values/dreams with empathy means that I also naturally listen to him with empathy to get to know his most inner needs/ desires/values/dreams. So, from my perspective, being honest and authentic is the most loving and valuable gift we can give to one another and the relationship.

Final Thoughts

Dear Reader. I hope you have come across something in this book that you can use. I hope that you have been inspired to give the upgrading of your Love another round. If there is anything I have learned on my long journey from 3D to 5D, it is that things take time. And that all the paths I have walked on through this journey have been and still are needed to be revisited again and again; each time to reclaim another little piece of myself. Again, and again. As we reach the end, I want to share some of my favourite words of wisdom with you that describes the process so well: *Still confused — but on a higher level.* The trip from 3D's to 5D's consciousness isn't a quick, straight, nor easy journey.

And that isn't so odd when we consider how many millennia humanity has lived in 3D. The patterns we are in the middle of transforming are deep-rooted within each and every one of us, and in the institutions, routines, and common knowledge we have based our lives on. So be patient with yourself. Meet yourself with Love, empathy, spaciousness, and understanding — even when your journey takes a detour or slows down. And remind yourself that there is a gift in everything — also in your so-called digressions and delays. *All is well* and exactly as it should be. Your soul, who is now taking the wheel in your life, knows this.

And when you let the soul take the wheel, things your ego cannot even imagine will happen. So, prepare yourself for a life where you come into deeper and deeper touch with your own truth. And prepare yourself for a truth that is much greater and more amazing than you expect. Prepare yourself for a life where you no longer have to make yourself smaller than you are. And for a life where you live committed to your soul's contracts and what your soul envisions for you.

Where you can give the gift to the world you have come to give. Your soul has surely whispered in your ear for a long time — through your most vivid feelings in your inner GPS. And now, as you step into 5D, there is no way around it. You can and will no longer ignore your soul's voice.

Because you now love and appreciate yourself as your creator loves and appreciates you. Now you feel which empty space your unique energy signature is due to fill in the world. Why your soul was created. And now you begin to fill that empty space by being wholly YOU. True to the messages you receive through your inner GPS, loving enough to listen to them, and brave enough to act on them. Because that is what true Love is; not a romantic perception of a conflict-free life on a rosy sky — but a clear, unconditional insistence in showing the world the true YOU. Strikingly and honestly — bravely and lovingly.

I wish you a delightful journey of reclaiming your divine, authentic truth, as *Love in the 5th Dimension* is. The truth and Love that you most likely have been longing for your entire life.

The time is now.

More Inspiration

A list of the authors and books I have mentioned:

- Anita Moorjani: *Dying To Be Me* and *What If This Is Heaven?*
- Louise Hay: *Trust Life, How to Love Yourself, Heal Your Body,* as well as other books and materials
- Abraham-Hicks: *Co-Creating at Its Best,* as well as other books and materials
- Matt Kahn: *Whatever Arises, Love That,* as well as other books and materials
- Marshall Rosenberg: *Nonviolent Communication,* as well as other books and materials
- Mary O'Malley: *The Gift of Our Compulsions*
- Mira Kelley: *Beyond Past Lives*
- Riane Eisler: *The Chalice and the Blade*
- Margit Madhurima Rigtrup: *Det Intelligente Hjerte* (only available in Danish)
- Pam Grout: *Thank & Grow Rich*
- Anja Steensig: *Book of Solace*
- Julia Cameron: *The Artist's Way*
- Ianneia Meldgaard: *Anerkendende Kommunikation - med empatien som vejviser* (only available in Danish)
- Ianneia Livia Silke Meldgaard: *At Vågne* (only available in Danish)

Guided Exercises and Meditations

Several of the book's exercises can be found as guided audio files on the webshop *empoweryou.dk* (currently only available in Danish):

- *Guided Exercise in Self-empathy*
- *Find Your Personal Love Declaration* — an expansion of Matt Khan's *I Love You* mantra
- *The Garden of Forgiveness* — the same exercise as this book's *The Garden of Liberty*
- *Attuning Your Send-and-Receive Station*

For more information, go to SHOP and then Guided Meditations. You can buy the files separately, as well as the four in the multipack Love in the 5th Dimension, which you then get for half the price.

Under Meditations in the shop, you can also find other guided audio files that each will help you elevate your vibrations in their own ways.

Online Courses

On the *empoweryou.dk* webshop, you can also find online courses to dive deeper into the themes of this book (currently only available in Danish):

- *Learn to Love Yourself — and create more Love in your life*
- *Forgiveness — set yourself and others free*
- *Gratitude — tap into a frequency of abundance and miracles*

These three online courses are purchased together under the title *The Fundamental Pack to the 5th Dimension* (in Danish: *Grundpakken til 5. Dimension*) where you then save some money compared to buying them all individually.

And you can find the big online course which builds on the five keys to reclaiming your power:

- *Manifest Your Life's Dream — create the life your soul desires with the Law of Attraction*

For more information on the courses, go to SHOP and then *Courses — Lectures — Books* and look around. In the same category you can also find video lectures about several of this book's topics.

Empowering Songs for the Soul

On ianneia.com you will find my two albums *Heart Choice* and *Marble & Feathers*, each with eleven *Empowering Songs for the Soul*, all tuned in 432 hz. Soft Nordic Jazz with lyrics in English. You can listen, read about the songs and buy them if you want. They can be purchased digitally as download. Click on BUY MUSIC in the menu.

Many of the songs are also uploaded on my YouTube channel *ianneia music*.

About the Author

Ianneia Livia Silke Meldgaard is a spiritual teacher, author and songwriter from Denmark. In her company Empower You she helps humans to navigate the great shift from 3rd to 5th Dimension that we currently are experiencing on Planet Earth.

Ianneia's own journey from 3rd to 5th Dimension started 30 years ago with a personality programmed with over-responsibility, self-critic and a big focus on giving Love to everyone else but herself. The journey has today resulted in a life based on soul-contact, authenticity and a deep inner knowing that true compassion for others comes from our ability to love ourselves unconditionally.

Most of the tools that Ianneia offers on www.empoweryou.dk are currently in Danish. This book is the first in English. Yet the lyrics in the Empowering Songs for the Soul in soft Nordic Jazz style are in English. Listen and learn more about the songs on www.ianneia.com or on Ianneia Music on YouTube.

Acknowledgements

THANK YOU to my mom and dad, who wandered on the path of the big plan for Planet Earth before me. Thank You for creating the perfect conditions for me to reclaim Love and the truth of who I really am.

THANK YOU to my wonderful family for going on this journey with me in this special time where big things are happening on Planet Earth. Thank You for what each of you has taught me about Love. It hasn't always been easy, but I feel Love becomes deeper and more alive at every bump in the road. Thank you for your openness and honesty.

THANK YOU to Torkild Clausen for beta reading and the invaluable feedback that helped make the book more reader-friendly. Thank You for taking the time to do so in the middle of your own activities.

THANK YOU to all of you who have attended my courses and lectures, bought my online courses and guided meditations, and shown me the trust in using me as your personal coach. Your feedback and reflections are priceless to me in my efforts to present material that makes sense and makes a difference for people who seek help in navigating the big energy shift on Earth.

THANK YOU to all of my friends—both to those skeptical of my views on everything and those who partly agree. It all contributes with valuable inspiration for my understanding of the essence of life and Love.

THANK YOU to Evita Ditlevsen and Steinar Ditlevsen for the collaboration in translating this book from Danish to English, so it can continue its journey out into the big world, as it wished from the start. It was a long process, but I feel we ended up with a sensitive translation that matches the original vibe in the book.

THANK YOU to Kim and Sinclair Macleod and Rachel Hessin from Indies Author World who helped with proofreading and international publishing of the book. It was such a relief for me to find you, since getting the book out into the big world was a task that I nearly couldn't comprehend, to be honest. To be guided to you by Divine Love (through the author Eva Andrea) was a gift that I am very, very grateful for. To be a member of your community lifted the weight off my shoulders and made it a wonderful and light process filled with confidence and Love.

THANK YOU to all of the spiritual leaders that have come before me, both to you who I have mentioned in this book and all of you I haven't. And there are many. You have been my light on this path and what has made me continue through the dark and difficult times. Thank You for your absolutely invaluable inspiration.

THANK YOU to all of the angels and spiritual beings that work in, with, and through me. Thank You for your inspiration and support; with this book and through my whole life. I know that your presence and help is omnipresent and more comprehensive than I am aware of, and I am deeply grateful. Without you, I would never have managed the earthly life's challenges with a smile.

THANK YOU, Divine Love, for choosing me to express yourself through. Thank You for the help I have received in opening myself to your messages. And Thank You for the healing I have received through the making of this book.

And THANK YOU, dear Reader, for choosing to invest your time and money in this book. Thank You for coming all the way here at the last page. The more humans that choose to reclaim Love, the better—and the quicker we can turn around the energy on our wonderful planet.

THANK YOU.